Your
Horoscope
2021

....

Aries

21 March – 20 April

igloobooks

igloobooks

Published in 2020
by Igloo Books Ltd
Cottage Farm
Sywell
NN6 0BJ
www.igloobooks.com

Copyright © 2019 Igloo Books Ltd
Igloo Books is an imprint of Bonnier Books UK

0820 001
2 4 6 8 10 9 7 5 3 1
ISBN 978-1-83852-315-2

Written by Belinda Campbell and Denise Evans

Cover design by Simon Parker
Edited by Bobby Newlyn-Jones

Printed and manufactured in China

CONTENTS

....

INTRODUCTION
. . . .

This 15-month guide has been designed and written to give a concise and accessible insight into both the nature of your star sign and the year ahead. Divided into two main sections, the first section of this guide will give you an overview of your character in order to help you understand how you think, perceive the world and interact with others and – perhaps just as importantly – why. You'll soon see that your zodiac sign is not just affected by a few stars in the sky, but by planets, elements, and a whole host of other factors, too.

The second section of this guide is made up of daily forecasts. Use these to increase your awareness of what might appear on your horizon so that you're better equipped to deal with the days ahead. While this should never be used to dictate your life, it can be useful to see how your energies might be affected or influenced, which in turn can help you prepare for what life might throw your way.

By the end of these 15 months, these two sections should have given you a deeper understanding and awareness of yourself and, in turn, the world around you. There are never any definite certainties, but with an open mind you will find guidance for what might be, and learn to take more control of your own destiny.

THE CHARACTER OF THE RAM

· · · · · · · · · · · · · · · · · ·

First in the zodiac year, first to get up in the morning, first to lend a helping hand and probably first on school sports days; Arians are a bundle of magnetic energy and quick-fire ideas. They tend to be the charismatic leaders of their pack, even if they don't volunteer themselves for the job. Whatever adventure Arians choose to chase after, there will always be a queue of admiring followers turning to these lively trendsetters for inspiration. Arians are aspirational and unparalleled in their zest for life, creative ideas and ability to get what they want.

Born in spring at the start of the equinox, the life and energy of Arians is palpable. It germinates in their abundance of ideas, flowers in their extrovert behaviour and bursts into life through their sometimes-impulsive actions. For Arians, the beginning of any venture is where their excitement lives and, sadly, often also dies. Whilst Arians thrive on beginning projects, whether it's starting up a business or learning a new craft, they don't always have the patience to see it through, leaving a path of half-painted canvases, unfinished novels and dust-gathering roller skates in their wake. It's not that Arians are ones to give up as such, far from it, but their childlike energy and impulsiveness can often become an impatient restlessness if a certain endeavour isn't going their way as quickly as they'd like it to. When one has as many fantastic ideas as Arians do, it's easy to understand why they may choose to ditch one enterprise to pursue another newer and 'greener' one. Although this quick-burning fire of interest can be problematic in love for Arians, resulting in short-lived lusts, their dependability is generally what they are better known for. When a problem occurs and someone suggests 'I know a person who can help with that', that person is likely to be an Arian.

THE RAM

Despite being born in springtime, there's not too much that's lamb-like about Arians! The Ram is known for being headstrong, and uses its impressive horns to settle arguments until it finally wins. Arians do not like losing an argument and so rarely will stop until they eventually win. It all comes back to being first because, as Arians would argue, what other outcome is there? This fighting quality has its pros and cons. Professionally, especially with those who are self-employed, the competitive, cardinal nature of Arians can be a vital characteristic for coming out top. It's important for Arians to be aware of their combative nature in their personal relationships too. Knowing how to identify when a win or loss for someone else is the same for them is vital to keeping any relationship happy and long-standing. The Ram is wild, ruling and sometimes angry, and it's these shared qualities that can make Arians so alluring to others, and viewed as a challenge or a chore to keep up with.

MARS

It's probably no surprise that the fiery red planet of
Mars rules Aries. Named after the Roman god of war, Mars,
like the Aries sign, is often associated with passion and rage.
However, Arians, like war, can demonstrate strategy and
discipline just as much as they cause destruction and chaos.
Whilst Aries and Mars are closely linked to being red-hot and
ready to win a fight, there is more to both these parties than a
steamy appearance. Once past the attractive, bold-red of Mars,
it's key to note its comparatively small size in the solar system
and its proximity to Earth. These attributes make Mars known
as an inner or 'personal' planet. Similarly, whilst there may be
a lot to see on the surface of the charismatic, sociable side of
Arians, one might be mistaken for thinking that's all there is.
Despite being primarily extroverted, Arians tend to internalise
their deepest thoughts and feelings. They like to keep their
private lives just that, private. The apparent closeness but
inner mysteries of this planet and sign may be one of the
reasons why humankind is so captivated with the red planet
and Aries.

ELEMENTS, MODES
AND POLARITIES

Each sign is made up of a unique combination of three
defining groups: elements, modes and polarities. Each of these
defining parts can manifest themselves in good and bad ways
and none should be seen as a positive or a negative – including
the polarities! Just like a jigsaw puzzle, piecing these groups
together can help illuminate why each sign has certain
characteristics and help us find a balance.

ELEMENTS

Fire: Dynamic and adventurous, signs with Fire in them can be extroverted. Others are naturally drawn to them because of the positive light they give off, as well as their high levels of energy and confidence.

Earth: Signs with the Earth element are steady and driven with their ambitions. They make for a solid friend, parent or partner due to their grounded influence and nurturing nature.

Air: The invisible element that influences each of the other elements significantly, Air signs will provide much-needed perspective to others with their fair thinking, verbal skills and key ideas.

Water: Warm in the shallows and freezing as ice. This mysterious element is essential to the growth of everything around it, through its emotional depth and empathy.

MODES

Cardinal: Pioneers of the calendar, cardinal signs jump-start each season and are the energetic go-getters.

Fixed: Marking the middle of the calendar, fixed signs firmly denote and value steadiness and reliability.

Mutable: As the seasons end, the mutable signs adapt and give themselves over gladly to the promise of change.

POLARITIES

Positive: Typically extroverted, positive signs take physical action and embrace outside stimulus in their life.

Negative: Usually introverted, negative signs value emotional development and experiencing life from the inside out.

ARIES IN BRIEF

The table below shows the key attributes of Arians.
Use it for quick reference and to understand more about this fascinating sign.

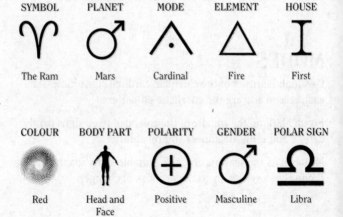

SYMBOL	RULING PLANET	MODE	ELEMENT	HOUSE
The Ram	Mars	Cardinal	Fire	First

COLOUR	BODY PART	POLARITY	GENDER	POLAR SIGN
Red	Head and Face	Positive	Masculine	Libra

ROMANTIC RELATIONSHIPS

· · · · · · · · · · · · · · · · ·

Warm, devouring, dangerous and exciting, the Aries element of Fire perfectly enlightens a potential spouse as to what the fast-burning love of an Arian can feel like. To some, the attraction of Arians is obvious, which is why there will often be a queue lining up. For others, the liveliness and spontaneity of Arians can be too hot to handle. The difficulty with finding someone that thinks the Arian free spirit is inspiring rather than tiring is perhaps why they are not best known for having long-term relationships. Arians can find the start of romantic relationships exciting but short-lived if they find themselves unmatched in passion and energy.

For a long-term relationship to work, Arians must continue to feel free – free to follow their ambitions, to act on their spontaneity and to roam where their hearts desire. A partner for an Arian is someone who will acknowledge the need for adventure, as well as the Arian desire for independence. It's essential for an Arian's partner to have separate interests, not only to keep the Arian satisfied but also to not lose themselves. Arians are cardinal, which means they initiate the zodiac calendar and commonly initiate their romantic relationships. When Arians hold a flame for someone, they do not make a secret of it and are quick to act.

Not everyone has the same energy and vigour as Arians; in fact some pride themselves on being the best. So how can they find an equal? Is an Arian only suited to another Arian? Although some feel that fire can only be fought with fire, this obvious solution may not be the best partnership of elements.

Regardless of signs, what Arians appreciate in a partner is someone who challenges them, shows a desire to share in their passions and, most importantly, brings humour into their lives.

ARIES: COMPATIBILITY 3/5

When a Fire sign meets Fire, there is sure to be lots of heat between the two. Whilst this could make for an exciting start, which both partners are sure to relish, it may be that they burn too brightly together and end up scalding each other. Both masculine and Fire signs, these two are likely to share characteristics like leadership and ambition and will encourage one another to achieve their full potentials. Whilst passions and interests are likely to be shared, two Rams could end up butting heads too frequently to form a harmonious romance.

TAURUS: COMPATIBILITY 3/5

The Bull and the Ram may look like two headstrong individuals doomed to clash, but they actually have the potential for a sensual relationship. Whilst their passions for each other are intense, this couple will need to keep a reign on their potential stubbornness and desire to win in order to form a lasting relationship outside of the sheets. The Taurean can be guilty of possessiveness, which the free-spirited Arian may struggle with. However, with a joint love of nature and being outdoors, this passionate duo could find their Eden together.

GEMINI: COMPATIBILITY 4/5

Though very different in their approaches to relationships, these two positive signs can bring out the very best in one another. Communication is key for any relationship and the Geminian's talkative nature can help the Arian vocalise their dreams and ideas. These two can form an intellectual bond that lays a strong foundation for their love. The Twins and Ram are both guilty of starting projects and not finishing them which can extend to their relationship with each other, but their similarities and positive natures are likely to still see them part as friends if the romance extinguishes.

CANCER: COMPATIBILITY 1/5

This pair shares opposite characteristics that don't always attract, sadly. A homely creature, the Cancerian may find the Arian's adventurous roaming too uncomfortable and unsettling. Conversely, the Arian will not thrive in this relationship if constricted or held back in any way by the Cancerian. However, these Water and Fire signs are true opposites, and therefore can stand to learn a great deal from one another. In particular, the Cancerian can teach the Arian to be more considered before acting, whilst the Arian can teach the Cancerian to be less worrisome.

LEO: COMPATIBILITY 2/5

Arians are used to being first, but they'll have to learn to share the spotlight and decision-making if they fall for this leader of the jungle. These two signs should recognise clearly their similarities, and therefore know just how to advise and support one another in reaching their goals. With the Leonian led by the heart and the Arian by the head, arguments can be a roaring battlefield when these two don't see eye to eye. Ego and pride will need to be kept in check on both sides if this relationship is to go the distance.

VIRGO: COMPATIBILITY 4/5

There's not a lot that's similar about how an Arian and Virgoan think and approach their daily decisions. The Arian rushes in excitedly to almost everything, whereas the Virgoan needs to exhaust all the facts and options first. The Arian can teach the Virgoan the benefits of not getting too bogged down with decisions, and the Virgoan can teach the Arian the equal importance of noticing the smaller details in life. When these two team up, they will understand that they are very, very different, and will likely admire those differences in one another.

LIBRA: COMPATIBILITY 5/5

A polarity is complementary for any star-sign pairing. For an Arian, a Libran is the yin to their yang, the Sun to their Moon, the wind to their fire. Libra is an Air sign, and can make the Arian's flames burn that much brighter. The Libran is best known for bringing harmony and balance into the world, and can make an ideal partner for the often-combative Arian. In this partnership of opposites, each can learn from the other in areas that they are lacking, with the Libran encouraging the Arian to communicate, and the Arian inspiring the Libran into action.

SCORPIO: COMPATIBILITY 2/5

If it's passion that an Arian desires in a relationship, a Scorpian could be the perfect sign for romance. However, this match might be too controlling and combative for long-term happiness. Both ruled by the planet Mars, these two may come into this relationship armed and ready to fight. The Scorpian's controlling and jealous tendencies could be a source of many explosive fights. If this Fire and Water sign can work out a balance of control and ease the Scorpian lover's jealousy, then they could have a steamy relationship rather than being left hot and bothered.

SAGITTARIUS: COMPATIBILITY 5/5

It will be a sure sign of Cupid's work if an Arian gets struck by one of the Sagittarian archer's arrows. This couple's compatibility is high due to their matching positivity and lively personalities. The Arian may have finally found their true match in the risk-taking Sagittarian. With a shared love of travel, there's unlikely to be any Arian adventure that the Sagittarian would pass up on. These two are go-getters and, if they can find shared interests, are an ideal match of two pioneering signs running off into the sunset together.

CAPRICORN: COMPATIBILITY 3/5

A cynical Capricornian is not an obvious lover for an ambitious Arian, but shouldn't necessarily be ruled out entirely as a potential partner. The Capricornian usually takes much longer to size up a partner than the quick-working Arian, so patience will need to be exerted if this challenging relationship is to work. Like with any partnership in life, their differences can become their strengths. They should, however, be mindful of not wanting to change one another. Instead, the Capricornian and Arian should strive to make the other a better, more well-rounded person.

AQUARIUS: COMPATIBILITY 3/5

Two signs known for their admirable quality of being a good friend to all, an Arian and Aquarian should have a good solid foundation of friendship to base their romantic relationship on. This coupling of Air and Fire will always make for a fuelled relationship. Independence is key for keeping the Aquarian lover happy, so the Arian should be careful with trying to control the relationship or forcing the Aquarian to commit too soon. Whilst these two signs have many things in common, it will be discovering each other's differences that will be essential in keeping both partners interested in this relationship.

PISCES: COMPATIBILITY 2/5

A dreamy Piscean and action-lead Arian can learn a lot from one another, if they can find the impetus to do so. The Piscean often fears delving into the deep end of desires, generally choosing to back other's dreams over their own. The Arian will want to help the Piscean reach their full potential, but may unintentionally upset their extremely sensitive lover. However, the Piscean can use the same emotional side to offer much-needed support to the Arian, who often forgets to pause for thought. Together, they could form a considered connection, deeper than most.

FAMILY AND FRIENDS

....

Born in the first house of the zodiac calendar, symbolising the self and personality, Arians are known for their individuality. So where does that leave their family and friends? Arians love to offer both practical and physical support; putting up a shelf, booking a house viewing, mowing the lawn, getting people out of bed for marathon training (that they may or may not have signed everyone up for!). Arians are first to help others, and can be extremely encouraging and invested in seeing those closest to them realise goals. Family and friends will appreciate having Arians in their lives and acknowledge the positive influence they bring.

As siblings, Arians can be aspirational figures that their brothers and sisters look up to. This idolisation can manifest itself in numerous ways, such as copying their hairstyles or borrowing their clothes. Just be sure to ask Arians first before taking their things to avoid sparking their temper. Should Arians wish to start their own family and have children of their own, their approach to parenting will be fun and energetic. Arians will have no problem running around after young children, keeping up with their endless energy and behaving like big kids themselves. The ever-changing demands of parenthood would likely suit Arians by keeping them challenged, whilst satisfying their childlike and curious nature.

Arians do well in polar relationships, where others supply traits in which they themselves are lacking. However, what might be most important for any successful bond with Arians is having common interests. Sport is likely to be an area where Arians have hobbies, and they will often meet friends this way.

Whether it's joining a sports club or competing in events, Arians' love for physical hobbies will steer them towards finding people with those similar interests.

Another key characteristic of Arians is their need for freedom. This craving for independence will mean that travel is usually prevalent, whether it is for work or pleasure. This love of travel can mean that Arians have a far-reaching global network of family and friends. If Arians find that their work takes them away, it's key to seek close friendships where both sides have a strong sense of independence and will not feel abandoned. Life-loving Sagittarians and individualist Aquarians can make the best family and friends for any fast-paced Arians.

Friends of Arians will know that they are always in, whatever the plan. Their enthusiasm is instant and uplifting. Arians aren't likely to decline offers of fun, which can prove troublesome when they later realise they have double-booked themselves – again. Beware of being bumped to the rejection list if an Arian finds a better offer elsewhere. It's nothing personal. Arians often cancel plans without thinking they may be upsetting friends and family by doing so.

MONEY AND CAREERS

. . . .

Being a particular star sign will not dictate certain types of career, but it can help identify potential areas for thriving in. Conversely, to succeed in the workplace, it is just as important to understand strengths and weaknesses to achieve career and financial goals.

Arians are driven more by goals than money, which for some individuals may be one and the same, but in most cases will overlap in some ways. When someone succeeds in their professional field, which Arians generally do, being a high earner usually comes with the territory. So even if money was not the end goal for Arians, it is usually a by-product of success and passion.

Arians are typically competitive and overflowing with energy, which, if channelled at an early age, can make sports an obvious career path. Some Arians prefer the competition and sociability of team sports, and may choose to follow in the footsteps of many famous Arian footballers. Other Arians prefer the constant competition of self-improvement, and find running a more satisfactory sport – just like Olympic gold medallist Mo Farah.

Arians are self-starters. This go-getter initiative may materialise itself as a crowdfunding project, a hobby that turns into a business idea, or a mini side project that turns into a profitable company. Whatever career ladder Arians climb, they will scale it quickly and always reach the top of their profession. That is, of course, as long as the job at hand is able to satisfy their ambition, and Arians can see that their frequent ideas are being listened to and acted upon.

A job in which Arians feel stagnant or stifled is not one they will stay in for any great length of time. Arians work best when they have freedom, be it creatively or by working flexible hours, and may struggle to satisfy this need for independence in more traditional workplaces. Self-employment options may be a better fit for this me-first sign, allowing them to be their own boss, dictate their own hours and free themselves from the nine to five.

In a modern world of online influencers, such as Arians Casey Neistat and Zoe Sugg, the sky's the limit for pioneering individuals who aren't afraid to go after what they want. This digital age is perhaps the most exciting era for Arians, as it has given them an outlet that lets them work nomadically from coffee shops or mountaintops.

If drawn to a more traditional workspace, the me-first attitude will need to be dialled down. Lessening the need to constantly win and learning to be able to compromise is essential learning for Arians if they are to thrive – which fundamentally is what they want! That being said, any team that contains one or more Arians is likely to come out on top. Arians are practical problem solvers and are first to help colleagues find the best solutions. This makes them generally very popular and an asset to any company.

As with family, colleagues cannot be chosen. Therefore, it can be advantageous to use star signs to learn about their key characteristics and discover the best ways of working together. Geminians can make for a helpful colleague by encouraging Arians to see a project from an alternative viewpoint. Geminians are also champion communicators, and can connect to Arians on an intellectual level and help them verbalise their ideas. Arians share a desire of winning with their Fire sign relation, Leo. However, just like close families, these two know how to fight better than anyone and can make for argumentative teammates. As with any successful relationship, Arians should try to exercise patience and take a leaf out of the Geminian book about how best to communicate with colleagues or customers in order to thrive in professional endeavours.

HEALTH AND
WELLBEING
··················

Arians are known for being one of the strongest and healthiest signs in the zodiac calendar. All associations with this sign, lively Fire plus combative Mars mixed with the headstrong Ram, can equate to the makings of an energetic individual. It's important that Arians find ways of positively expelling this natural energy, and one of the ways this can be done effectively is through sports. Arians are unlikely to be satisfied simply by running out their energy on a treadmill in the gym, rather this sign is more likely to enjoy team sports such as football or basketball to complement their social and competitive nature. Other Arians that feel the ruling of Mars more keenly may find that martial arts are their passion, like fellow Arian Jackie Chan.

Represented by the zodiac symbol of the Ram, this headstrong animal perfectly symbolises the ferocity and wildness in which Arians charge after what they desire most. The Ram is known not only for its strength, but also for having unbelievable balance on dizzyingly high and rocky terrains. Which may be why some Arians find that their sense of adventure leads them to try thrill-seeking sports that rely on strength and balance, such as rock climbing, mountain biking or even aerial acrobatics. Whether Arians focus their abundance of energy and aptitude for action into a particular sport, their love for adventure is likely to have them craving after some sort of lifestyle in the great outdoors, whether that's hiking or wild swimming.

Physical activity is well suited to Arians, not only for the obvious benefits of keeping their bodies physically healthy but also for their mental wellbeing. This highly charged sign needs a positive outlet for releasing their excess energy. If Arians feel a fight boiling up in them they would do well to throw their trainers on, step out of their front door into some fresh air and just run it out. Chances are, they'll feel much better for having expelled some of their energy, and especially for applying it to something constructive as this is what this positive sign naturally craves.

It's key for Arians to stay active in an area that brings them joy to avoid frustration, however, this sign should be wary of pushing themselves too much and too quickly, as they could end up injuring themselves in the process. Slowing down, weighing up risks and taking a moment to simply breathe can help Arians maintain a positive state of mind. They would do well to try incorporating more meditative hobbies into their active lifestyles. Yoga will help stretch out overworked muscles and mediation will help calm a warrior-like approach to life, and bring a much-needed breath of tranquillity. Arians are traditionally linked to the head, and may find that they suffer from headaches more acutely and frequently or conversely not at all. Either way, if Arians can periodically pause and calm their active mind and body, they could find it brings a clearer focus that leads to long-term health and happiness.

Aries

. . . .

DAILY FORECASTS
for 2020

OCTOBER

. . . .

Thursday 1st

October starts with the Full Moon in your sign. You may
want to look back at the Aries New Moon shortly after the
Spring Equinox and think about all the things that have
changed since then. What is highlighted now is self versus
other. Reflect on how this is balanced.

Friday 2nd

Venus moves out of the area of your inner king or queen and
moves into your area of health, diet and day-to-day life. She
will support your changes here, and it will be easier for you to
consider what is of value to you and what is not. Take a look
at how you look after yourself in terms of food, exercise and
mental health. Could you make a few small improvements?

Saturday 3rd

This Saturday is made for wellness. Treat yourself and your
loved ones well, either by going to a spa, taking a bath or going
out for dinner. Have some delicious food. Days like this are
about recharging and even being lazy. Reflect on your mental
and spiritual well-being as well as your physical well-being.

Sunday 4th

Your emotions are likely to be focused on yourself today, while
your mind may be focused upon others. As you know, the key
is to see both as equally important. One of the biggest tasks
you face is finding a balance here. Today is one more step
towards it. Perhaps write some lists if it helps you to see the
bigger picture.

Monday 5th

There is a stable and solid energy. Pluto also agrees the foundation is good for now and moves direct. It is unlikely that anything new will come up for the remainder of this year, but everything should be solidified and your transformation may become more visible.

Tuesday 6th

Communication should be in full swing today. There will probably be a lot of good talks and most of them will have an element of depth. You have no interest in idle chatter, so draw a line if someone approaches you on that level. Today may offer some insights and revelations.

Wednesday 7th

If you stay curious today then you may receive some surprising news. You will want to investigate what you find out, but be careful that others are not left feeling uncomfortable by your curiosity. Make it clear that your intention is to fully understand the situation, not to gossip about it. Be aware of the personal boundaries of others.

Thursday 8th

You should feel ready to ponder and reflect on some of the insights and information you received recently, but all from the comfort of home. Find your favourite blanket, make a pot of tea and snuggle up. It's wonderful to end the day like this. Use a journal or notebook, or put on your favourite music, if it helps.

Friday 9th

Pluto has a message for Mars retrograde, so you will find out what is needed to make an important transformation visible to the outside world. It concerns how you represent yourself and how others see you. Consider how you see yourself and how you want others to see you. What changes do you feel need to be made here?

Saturday 10th

Venus is finally having a good conversation with Uranus. He is keen to notice that she brings some important values to the table, so this could well be about your food and diet. As Uranus is currently in a ground-breaking mode it is possible to plant some seeds. Maybe even literally. Think about your physical health and perhaps shake things up in terms of the meals you have regularly.

Sunday 11th

A Sun and Jupiter day today, but this time they are not so aligned as they were earlier on in the year. However, they like each other enough that they will find common ground. In this case, it is to find alignment with how the world sees you and your relationships. That should be of equal importance too. Let your thoughts reflect on everything you have learned and considered over the last couple of weeks.

Monday 12th

A Leo Moon arrives, bringing time for creative expression or playfulness. You should make good use of it in any way you can, as it will make you feel good and give your Mars energy an outlet. If you are craving anything now, it is probably to release some energy. Perhaps consider an evening get-together with friends, family or even colleagues to kick-start the week.

Tuesday 13th

The Virgo Moon will ask if you have begun your daily tasks. If you have, well done. If you haven't, start right away. The Sun is now facing Mars and challenges your actions. Remember the key is to find balance in all relationships. Are you fulfilling your duties at home and with friends as well as work? Maybe check in with your loved ones this evening.

Wednesday 14th

If you feel low on energy today it is probably because we are in the balsamic phase of the Moon. If you found something during the last few days that you would like to investigate more deeply, Mercury is making it happen.

Thursday 15th

The Sun and Pluto are not on the same page today, but at least the Sun has some support now. You will have to consider many things during the upcoming lunar cycle to bring things into harmony. There's nothing wrong with starting now, so look forwards as well as backwards as today draws to a close.

Friday 16th

Happy New Moon in Libra. As this happens in your opposite sign, you can consider it the second most important New Moon for you. You are currently working on your relationships and this lunar cycle is here to support you. You will come to terms with many things during this time, so welcome it with open arms and an open mind.

Saturday 17th

Mercury has retrograded to Scorpio, putting intimacy, passion and desire in the spotlight. This retrograde is also contributing to your new personal relationship approach. It is all working inside of you now, but imagine how much will have changed for the better when you are done. Be reflective and flexible to make this change smoother.

Sunday 18th

Today will likely bring up a challenge, but maybe also a way to tackle it. It is also possible that you'll find some resources that can help you achieve your legacy goals. It is not a bad day, you just have to take on the challenge. Be ready to take an extra moment to think things through and consider your options.

Monday 19th

Jupiter is today's guide, so you should feel full of positivity. He has an argument with Mars, as well as a lovely conversation with Venus. This is likely to leave you cautious about integrating day-to-day changes into your identity, but do not fear them. These changes will support your expansion.

Tuesday 20th

Today's deep ponderings may be stirred up by a surprising insight. What are your thoughts about property, possessions and resources? Does everything need to be merged in a relationship? Are you willing to share? What are your boundaries? There will be things to consider deeply, today.

Wednesday 21st

Make this Wednesday fully focused on what you want to achieve. Venus has a good talk with Pluto, so things are moving forward – whether you notice them or not. This progression is probably not happening in the way you expected, but embrace it all the same. Be patient and trust that it will eventually work out for the best.

Thursday 22nd

Scorpio season is here. If you look out of the window you will find that we are in the midst of autumn, a season of deep transformation. If you look inside yourself, you will see you are in the midst of a deeply transformative period. Keep putting in the work and results will come your way. Sometimes you must give something up or shed old skin for a proper transformation to take place.

Friday 23rd

Today is a good day to connect and it's made for big gatherings. You're less likely to take things personally today and are able to hear more than what is said my employing your insight, which should be on top form. You can surprise others with your current super powers and should make good use of them.

Saturday 24th

It feels like Venus is doing nothing other than talking to planets in Capricorn. She's actually busy connecting the dots on everything you have implemented so far, and getting the green light for making changes. Patience may not always come to you naturally or easily, but try to focus on employing this virtue today.

Sunday 25th

Mercury is deep in the Sun today, ready to receive orders for his new cycle. Interestingly, the meeting takes place in the same spot where the Sun met Venus during her retrograde in 2018. That was exactly two years ago today. Can you make a connection? Looking back, did something happen on this day? Was a course of events set in motion? What's changed in the last two years?

Monday 26th

Today will see you focus on your emotions and how to make the dream of more love in this world a reality. Connect to your feelings and reserve a spot to think and drift away. Just a little. Don't be afraid to feel, today, and perhaps put this evening aside for some quiet downtime to accommodate these feelings.

Tuesday 27th

There is a good chance that today feels as dreamy as yesterday. Maybe you can go easy and put off the hands-on jobs until tomorrow? It is not so dreamy that you will fly away, but it is powerful enough to connect with. Reserve some time for meditation or a walk in the park. Be sure to make some room for yourself.

Wednesday 28th

The universe is supporting you by putting full focus on your balance between self and other. Mercury retrogrades back into Libra, Venus comes in from the other end and the Moon enters your sign. The solution is coming closer, just make sure that you're ready to receive it. Taking on a receptive and reflective mindset for the time being will do you no harm.

Thursday 29th

Today you feel yourself strongly. You are somebody who wants to act from honour, and for a cause. You need to stay true to yourself. You need to be authentic. It is not all about you, but you cannot lose yourself in a relationship either. Put your feet forward with certainty, and remember your recent lessons and reflections in all that you do today.

Friday 30th

Do you feel the energy building up? There might be some tension as you start the day, but it is just for today and in the evening things will ease. Remember to breathe and look forward to the weekend, and this will help to get you through. Have a relaxed night and save the partying for tomorrow.

Saturday 31st

Happy Halloween! Today comes with the Taurus Full Moon, which is sat on top of Uranus. If you go to a Halloween party, be sure to opt for the treat rather than the trick. It will save you from at least one of today's surprises. Be on your guard, but let yourself have fun. It could be a very interesting day.

NOVEMBER

. . . .

Sunday 1st

Today's energy is generally uncomplicated, because the Moon finds some stability with Jupiter. There could still be something in the woods, so awareness is key. Otherwise, it is a great day to connect, revel in any feelings of calmness which come your way and perhaps enjoy amazing food. Maybe pumpkin soup?

Monday 2nd

Monday morning starts slowly and you'll take time to engage fully. From midday onwards it gets busier and suddenly there is so much to do that you might lose your cool. Try to approach each job one at a time, whilst making notes. Otherwise, something important may slip through.

Tuesday 3rd

This should be a beautiful and optimistic day. You are able to connect with Mars, so you know what you want to do next. You are also able to bring harmony to your relationships. That's music to your ears, isn't it? It might take a little work and won't always be plain sailing, but stick with it.

Wednesday 4th

You've dug deeply enough, Mercury has excavated everything necessary and he is now moving direct. The Moon also crosses the north node today, giving you a glimpse of how it feels to finally move forwards. Your guide will soon return, and then there will be no more holding back. Do what you need to get by until then.

Thursday 5th

You may be tempted to stay at home today. Venus has an argument with the Moon about what she sees as fair and beautiful in your relationships, and you are asked to feel what is good and right for you. This might throw some tests or trials in your direction which will demand your attention. Don't think. Feel your way.

Friday 6th

Mars is having an argument with the Moon today. The Moon is also facing each of the Capricorn planets, Pluto, Jupiter and Saturn, which means you are busy. The purpose? It is all working towards your balance between these important points. So if today feels a little tough, be reassured that tomorrow looks brighter.

Saturday 7th

It's Saturday and also a Moon in Leo day. Let your inner king or queen come out this weekend and shower yourself in self-love. Today's motto should be, "I love myself". Say it aloud, and maybe even in front of a mirror, for maximum effect. Listen for what you need and try to give it yourself in abundance.

Sunday 8th

Stick to the self-love affirmation and stay away from drama today – no matter how tempting it is to get involved. Take a step back and retreat to a safe place if it helps. Try to enjoy being with, and giving love to, the people closest to you. They will appreciate it as much as you will.

Monday 9th

Today is about grounding something into reality, about finding harmony between Venus in her home and Mars in his. This is a balancing moment, as the wise Queen speaks to the receptive King. The harmony may need to be found in a relationship, in the workplace, or even within yourself. Open your heart today and you will be rewarded a thousand times.

Tuesday 10th

Mercury spends his last day in Libra and is ready to go back to Scorpio. After the meeting between Mars and Venus, he knows everything can continue to the next level. So what is the insight you took from yesterday? What is the greatest vision of a relationship that you want to bring into reality? Focus hard on what needs to be addressed.

Wednesday 11th

Today looks promising. You should still be focused on grounding everything and you connect to all the Capricorn planets as well. You know this all goes straight to your foundation. Can you feel how much is currently moving? Can you feel an excitement rising within? Take a moment to stop and take stock of how you're feeling and everything that's moving around you.

Thursday 12th

Not only is the Moon in your relationship house today, but it is also the final meeting of Pluto and Jupiter with Saturn watching over them. This time they find a way to connect all of their realms. The heaven and the underworld, your light and your shadow. It is such a powerful moment. Be mindful of things coming together, perhaps in unexpected ways.

Friday 13th

You might still be marvelling about current developments. Now you can align your feelings with everything and any concerns will quickly pass. Later, the Moon joins the Sun and Mercury in Scorpio so things line up for the next level. There is just one more thing needed. Try to make sure that you're ready for the next phase.

Saturday 14th

Mars moves direct, allowing you to look back at the intense amount of inner work you have done. Who do you see when you take a look in the mirror now? You should be very proud. From here on, life moves in one direction and one direction only – forwards. Try to find a way to reward yourself, today.

Sunday 15th

Sometimes the universe wastes no time, so here is the New Moon in Scorpio. It gives you the opportunity to go deeper and connect in a new way. What is the level of intimacy you want to have in your life? You can plant it now, and see how far it has grown by the Scorpio Full Moon next year. This is a good time to develop in more areas than just one.

Monday 16th

Maybe you could say that today is about the idea of a value and the reality of it. As long as that value is just a concept then it is good to have, but how much richer can you be if you implement it? Remember that this might not equate to financial value. Consider other values you hold dear.

37

Tuesday 17th

Something has to happen to make your idea a reality, and it
might just be an old belief that you can let go of. It may come
as a surprise that this belief is still within you, making it even
more important to become conscious of it and then release it.
It is no longer serving you. Be open to abandoning old luggage
you may not be aware you were still carrying, but still have
some sort of sentimental attachment to.

Wednesday 18th

You are focused today, and ready for achievements, but are
your actions in alignment? Try not to be impatient. It will
take a moment until you are back to full force as Mars, who
regulates your energy, has just started to move again. By
December, you will be back to full speed. Slow and steady is
the way for now.

Thursday 19th

When it comes to work, as well as how the world sees you and
your legacy, you may receive some appreciation today. Your
transformation starts to become visible, both to yourself and
those around you, but know that it needs a little more time
to unfold fully. It takes time for a caterpillar to emerge from a
chrysalis and display its full beauty as a butterfly.

Friday 20th

Now that you are back in your own energy again, you can play
around with some out-of-the-box thoughts. The combination
of the Moon, Uranus and Mercury feels tense, but it is
something you can use creatively. Who, if not you, would have
more fun lighting a creative spark that is entirely new? Have
fun with it.

Saturday 21st

Today should be interesting. The Moon is still in genius mode and is aligning with the north node in the direction we are all heading towards. The Sun sits in optimistic Sagittarius, so if you have a spark burning it will shoot it wherever you want. If you have a creative project underway, or plans for one in the near future, throw yourself into it now.

Sunday 22nd

Venus has brought you balance, a sense of equality and harmony. She has brought you all the beauty she can. Now she is also ready to move on from relationships in general to true intimacy. This is where the magic happens. Are you ready to get deep? When considering this, reflect on all the forms intimacy might take, and who with. This might mean more than a physically romantic relationship.

Monday 23rd

It is a day to once again connect with your innermost self, to meditate, dream and go easy on yourself. The energy is a good one, it is just more focused inwards than it is outwards. It is ultimately an energy that aligns to universal love. Getting to know yourself is essential to truly getting to know others and letting them get to know you.

Tuesday 24th

Yesterday's theme of universal love continues, with you pondering the most dreamy and intimate love possible. It may be love with a partner or with the world itself. It might have to do with family, friendship or simply being true to yourself. The residing message to take away from it all is that if you can dream it, you can do it.

Wednesday 25th

The Moon in Aries, Mars direct and the Sun in Sagittarius really fuels your energy. Use it to recharge and ponder of some of your beliefs. Which thoughts do you still want to act on, and which are you ready to let go? Today is an opportunity to reflect and look inwards if you haven't already been doing so this week; make sure you give yourself the time to do so.

Thursday 26th

It is another day of practising patience. You are ready to act and to move, and you will, but be aware that it is unlikely to be at your usual speed. Be assured that this is okay and part of the process. The change is here. It is happening and there is no need for you to rush. Trust on that.

Friday 27th

Venus faces Uranus, which means that you're likely to experience issues with intimacy or closeness at the moment, especially within relationships. With Venus and the sign of Taurus involved, it could concern physical pleasure or passion. The presence of Uranus implies that you should also be on your guard.

Saturday 28th

It should be an easy and flowing day. Daydream, relax or simply enjoy the afterglow of recent positives. At the least, have a bath, a massage or do something else that stimulates the senses while also relaxing you. Food is also good, but it is not the first choice today.

Sunday 29th

Can you feel the energy building up again? The energy is very grounded but you might also feel tired or even restless. Either way, you should expand your mind about the level of intimacy that is possible for you. How much more is available for you? Take some time to reflect, perhaps with a notebook if it helps you to concentrate your mind.

Monday 30th

November ends with a powerful day, specifically on a Full Moon lunar eclipse in Sagittarius. It all ties into a bigger scale and a theme you are working on. The Moon is illuminating your curiosity for the new and, in order to make way for it, you have to release some outdated beliefs. Be prepared to broaden your mind or have it broadened from outside sources.

DECEMBER

· · · · · · · · · · · · · · · · · ·

Tuesday 1st

Yesterday's Moon was close to the north node, but today it comes right on top of it. You'll receive more clarity on where to go, as Mercury comes into Sagittarius to consciously work on your belief system. Mercury is still behind the Sun, so it may take a while until it all makes sense. Make sure that you're patient and your mind is open.

Wednesday 2nd

The Moon highlights your home and family life. You may want to feel nurtured and you now know very well how to do it. Do whatever gives you comfort and makes you feel fully at home. It is also a good day to get in contact with your family or chosen family, as this will root you in the energy that you require from today.

Thursday 3rd

Not everything might be happy at home. If tension arises, just remember to respond differently. Mars retrograde was about acting differently and now you can put these new actions into play. You will be amazed at what new choices this opens up for you and your loved ones. You may need an extra moment to remember this and process the world around you in a slightly different way, but it will make all the difference.

Friday 4th

This is the last time for a while that you have to face an imbalance between your responsibilities and your world in this magnitude. That alone should give you enough fuel to make the final adjustments. There is also a Moon in Leo, so a sense of joy and happiness is available to you. Storms that come your way today should only be small and, if you take this into account, you should weather them with ease.

Saturday 5th

You should love today. You'll receive a maximum amount of fire and your actions, emotions and visions all line-up. You can feel the spirit again and Mars, your guide, is picking up speed so you feel almost back to normal. Try to open yourself up to a new source of energy and you'll quickly become refuelled this weekend.

Sunday 6th

You're likely feeling very positive, with a sense of excitement about all that could be possible. The world really needs you to share those feelings. Encounter people with love and your broadest smile and see how it echoes around. While you feel yourself rising, you should be able to lift a few others with you and increase the feeling further.

Monday 7th

The season and all that it brings may start to throw its challenges your way, but you can lessen the blows by being organised early. With preparation, you can spare yourself some time and stress later, and be ready for any surprises that might come your way.

Tuesday 8th

Hopefully, you are organised and able to set up everything perfectly. Do whatever you can today, even if it is still sixteen days until Christmas Eve. You will be busy with other things and today it will all flow. Make the most of the time that you have and make sure that everything is ready and how it needs to be.

Wednesday 9th

You may discover some beliefs about relationships in general, and a lack of harmony in the connection between your vision and your dreams. This isn't to say it isn't possible, only that you need another state of mind in order to make it possible. Use your strengths to see things differently when it comes to problem solving.

Thursday 10th

Venus is on the hunt. She finds something about intimacy that wants to be examined and transformed. It has rarely been so easy to just go and explore. Expect a passionate, and potentially unforgettable encounter, just be prepared for it to take shape in ways you might not expect.

Friday 11th

This is potentially a huge day of intensity and removal or reshaping of a major belief. These two aspects may be interlinked, but not necessarily. The Sun sits on the south node where she finds the riches of the past, but also the beliefs that brought you here. Those thoughts will not bring you to the future, so Mars just ends it right there.

Saturday 12th

Your actions are aligning with your future direction. You are able to go deeper into your own shadow to excavate more outworn beliefs, and you are sparking up with ideas about the future. Even though it is the balsamic Moon, you still have enough energy available and don't feel tired. Have compassion for those who do.

Sunday 13th

This day is full of festive spirit, yet you might feel that something else is brewing as Saturn reaches the final Capricorn degree again. You probably still have a lot to do, but are happy to focus your energy into something where the results are so apparent. The mountaintop is in sight.

Monday 14th

Happy New Moon in Sagittarius. It is the final New Moon this year, which sees you owning your fire and shooting it out into the world. There is uncharted territory to be covered and you are always pioneering in a new world. Come up with a big vision and make it happen. Being so close to the end of the year is no reason to slow down.

Tuesday 15th

Extra fire energy arrives as Venus joins the Sun and Mercury in Sagittarius. Venus is welcomed in Jupiter's home, making this a great day to meet others, wander around a Christmas market or plan your next holiday. However you choose to channel and expend this energy, the only thing that matters is that it beautifies your world.

Wednesday 16th

Dreams are my reality… that is the song the Moon would sing today as it connects with Pluto and the deep waters of Neptune. While the Moon is singing, Saturn is living on the edge of his mountain home in Capricorn. So, while you are daydreaming, tune into that feeling of a major shift. Today could offer something fantastic.

Thursday 17th

The Moon conjoins Jupiter, who is now on the final degree of Capricorn. Elsewhere, Saturn finally steps out of the door and into Aquarius. Now think back to the end of March when the Moon first arrived here. What has been relevant for you, and what have you been trying to anchor in? How is the situation different now? Today is a good time to reflect on the changes of the year.

Friday 18th

The Moon has crossed over to Aquarius and run right into Saturn, who is holding the door. You are now really focusing on these grand approaches and building a new world. This has just the right amount of adventure, importance and courage. A new mission beckons to you; seize it and dream big!

Saturday 19th

Jupiter is full of joy today because he knows it is his last day in Capricorn. The last day of restrictions. So whatever work you have to do today to finish something, do it. Once the step is taken you won't want to come back to finish and it would be a pity after all you have already worked through. Tick as many boxes on your to-do list as you can, today.

Sunday 20th

Today is somehow magical, thanks to Mercury meeting the Sun in the final degree of Sagittarius, hiding in the galactic centre. If you believe in a higher power, it will come into play today and aligns you to the highest good of all. If you don't, consider it a day to have this inner knowledge of being on the right path with everything being as it should be.

Monday 21st

Sit down. Take a breath. This is the day of the Winter Solstice. In the maximum darkness, Saturn and Jupiter meet to start an entirely new cycle with the promise of more light coming in, each step of the way. This is a time to sit still and quiet, if you can, and to take stock of the happenings around you, in time as well as space.

Tuesday 22nd

The last few days before Christmas are loaded with action. Do you want to honour tradition or start something new? It may be wise to choose what is easiest. Are you really ready to do it your way? Think carefully about how you implement these last few preparations and that they don't uproot all your hard work so far.

Wednesday 23rd

If you have decided to transform familiar traditions, you will need to act fast. Try to stay calm as you make last-minute changes and steady your nerves. The more you've tried to be organised and prepare this month, the more it will be its own reward. How much relaxation have you bought yourself?

Thursday 24th

After such a hectic year, relief comes in the form of the Moon in Taurus. You will be able to experience an atmosphere of comfort, peace and acceptance. It may seem too good to be true, but a restful and restorative Christmas awaits. Now is the time to take a deep breath, ready to breathe out a sigh of relief.

Friday 25th

Merry Christmas! Enjoy the festivities around you and being with loved ones, taking your time to be fully present in the moment. Indulge in the feast; the best of the best is on the table today. Just have a good time and let yourself go. Today is the one day of the year where imposing restrictions is truly punishing yourself for enjoyment.

Saturday 26th

Have a singalong or watch a movie today. The cosy energy is still available, so you can also make it a lazy day. If you are out to visit relatives, don't be surprised if they are more interested in board games than a snowball fight. Bask in the warm glow and enjoy the feeling of being surrounded by loved ones.

Sunday 27th

Interestingly enough, once the break is over, everyone is much more interested in connecting than before. This will keep you busy answering calls and catching up on messages. Nothing major is happening otherwise, so just connect. Today is a social day; enjoy making contact and keeping in touch.

Monday 28th

Curiosity is high. What will the new year bring and what surprises are coming up? What will ground you? These are the questions that might go around in circles in your head. The answer is that you don't know yet, but you are on the direct path to the future and it has a good chance to be amazing!

Tuesday 29th

It's the last Full Moon of the year, and a Full Moon in Cancer. This is the place where you have put a lot of effort in throughout 2020. You have successfully learnt to nurture yourself and be there for your family in a new way. Even more importantly, you have found emotional stability and independence from the outside world.

Wednesday 30th

As you reflect on the year behind, you find a balance between heart and mind while also reconnecting to the dream you want to carry forward. Connect to your emotions, and appreciate all that you have been through this year.

Thursday 31st

It is the final day of the year, and the Moon is still focusing on your emotions and your further transformation. You are constantly evolving and tomorrow is the next step. Take a moment to look back on how far you have come, this year and all the others, and consider how far you might still go. Have a good and blessed ride.

Aries

......

DAILY FORECASTS
for 2021

JANUARY

. . . .

Friday 1st

Happy New Year and welcome to 2021. Last year ended with a
Full Moon in your family sector. This illuminated issues with
your family of origin. Perhaps you had a clan gathering to
celebrate. You now have a lovely, creative, playful Moon to start
the year. Enjoy childhood memories today.

Saturday 2nd

Mars is in the final degrees of your sector of self. Is there
something you need to do for yourself that has been
neglected over the holidays? As your ruler, he urges you to be
assertive and to go after what you want. Find your voice and
speak your truth.

Sunday 3rd

Today you may need to check in with your health. Have
you overdone the food and drink recently? Take some time
today to detox, cleanse or simply tidy up your home. Fitness
regimes can be resumed, and you have a good chance of being
consistent with them now. Check your schedule, too.

Monday 4th

Are you feeling little foggy today? You may feel drawn to put
things in order, but there is a cloud over you. Neptune in your
sector of dreams is trying to whisk you away from your duties.
Try to stay grounded and do the daily grind, it will help.

Tuesday 5th

There may be some issues of control in the workplace. Perhaps you need to speak to the boss or another paternal figure. Keep your ears open and listen to good advice. At the same time, there may be some gossip flying around; do your best not to get drawn in.

Wednesday 6th

Today may well be a good time to assert yourself. Your ruler is about to leave his sign, so it is now is probably the best time to speak your mind. If you do not, you may miss out on an opportunity and will kick yourself. If you've been putting something off, seize the moment. Be active, do it now.

Thursday 7th

Mars settles into your finances and self-worth sector. You should find that things slow down a little now. You probably feel this is frustrating, but if you let Mars set the pace you cannot go wrong. Put that energy into sorting out your home environment and your finances.

Friday 8th

The Moon shifts into your sex, death and rebirth sector. This sector also deals with joint finances. You can feel more intense and emotional now. This makes you uncomfortable but is a trigger to guide you and take action. Something may need to end or be transformed now. What is it?

Saturday 9th

Planetary activity is quite high today. Mercury will move into your social sector and Venus spreads the love in your career. Be mindful that you walk your talk today as Mars and Mercury are squaring off. There may be some conflict or misunderstandings in your social groups.

Sunday 10th

You should feel more outgoing today and may seek entertainment through other cultures and philosophies. Mercury meets up with the first of the planets affecting your social sector this year. Saturn will teach you about boundaries and limits within your social groups. He can be harsh but fair. These are big lessons for you.

Monday 11th

Today Mercury meets Jupiter. Truth, justice and expansion will also be themes for your social activities this year. This is the time to get your friends lists in order and sort out who is good for you and who is not. Perhaps look to distance yourself from negative friendships. You will benefit highly if you listen.

Tuesday 12th

Be on the lookout for some shocks or surprises within your social groups, and your home and finances. Watch what you say, as the energy today can mean that you say the wrong thing to the wrong people. Check your financial resources and do not be tempted to impulse buy.

Wednesday 13th

A New Moon occurs today in your career sector. This is a great time to set late resolutions regarding your work and career. Look at the responsibilities you have. You may feel a childlike resistance or resentment towards them. Check again after this energy has passed.

Thursday 14th

You might feel like starting the weekend a little early. You are likely to connect with friends and there's a strong chance of a social gathering. Alternatively, you could be irritated and ready to start a revolution. Something has got you jumpy and you cannot sit still today; use that energy positively.

Friday 15th

The weekend is here and you feel the need to enjoy it with friends. This can also mean that you spend time on social media connecting with your wider tribe. You need to spend time or simply be with people who share your views now. Be ready to party.

Saturday 16th

Your mood slips into a dream state. What started as a great idea has now lost its pace. You might be changing your mind about someone or something. The best that you can do now is to retreat and spend time with your thoughts and dreams. Enjoy some precious time to yourself.

Sunday 17th

You may be caught up in fantastical thinking today. Try not to build castles in the sky. Take off the rose-tinted glasses. If you must use this energy, indulge in a good book or binge watch a TV show. There is an inner conflict between spending time with friends or at home. Choose wisely.

Monday 18th

The Moon comes into your sign. This makes you feel surer of yourself but be careful not to extend that to bossiness. Be your best self and get productive. Make lists and plans. There is a helpful connection to Saturn and Jupiter in your social sector.

Tuesday 19th

Communication is being helped by Mercury and you can get your point across easily. Just be aware that you may upset someone in the workplace. Your views may clash with the boss and you may need to back down. Harmony at work may be disrupted today.

Wednesday 20th

Tempers and tantrums may erupt today. Mars and Uranus meet, and the effect can be very volatile. This happens in your home and finance sector. There is a chance that you will overspend. Your self-worth could be threatened, and you will be called to defend yourself. Calm down and pause before reacting.

Thursday 21st

This is still an unsettled day for you. You must listen to your inner voice or, at the very least, the voices of friends who care for you. There may be stand-offs with authority or paternal figures. Mercury wants you to listen and not react, as this may affect your future.

Friday 22nd

Venus softens the edges of the recent antagonism. Pluto also steps in and takes control. Today you are being urged to spend time in your safe environment, whether that's at home or elsewhere. Soothe yourself with good food and music and switch off from bad atmospheres. Enjoy some time alone, today.

Saturday 23rd

This weekend would be a good time to catch up on odd jobs or little things which you've been putting off. Siblings and old friends can bring you joy. You may feel a desire to connect and be outgoing today but let that be with those who do not judge you. Aggression still boils below the surface.

Sunday 24th

The Sun meets Saturn today in your social sector. This will illuminate the message that Saturn has for you about boundaries and authority. Take heed at whatever comes to light today. Your emotions reach out to the future. What can you do to make that a better place for yourself?

Monday 25th

Mars and Jupiter are squaring off today. One wants action
in your home sector and the other needs truth, justice and
expansion. Jupiter makes everything bigger so be warned, if
action and aggression are still on your mind then it can get
out of hand. Use the Moon's energy today to comfort yourself.

Tuesday 26th

Your family sector is touched by the Moon now. You need to
feel nurtured and protected. Your inner child may be asking
you to slow down and step away from trouble. Maternal figures
will be a good influence today. Home-cooked foods will also
satisfy your need for comfort.

Wednesday 27th

There may be some control issues today. Enjoy soothing your
inner child but be careful that any influential maternal figures
do not try to manipulate you. You could be lulled into a false
sense of security so if a red flag appears, do something about it
and remove yourself.

Thursday 28th

A Full Moon in your creative sector highlights play time.
This can be a creative time where you allow yourself to enjoy
making art or just a mess. Your inner child needs protection
but also the freedom to express themselves. Laugh, play and
create. Do this as much as you're able, today.

Friday 29th

This should be a highly beneficial day. If you are still in inner child mode, you may wish upon a star as Jupiter and the Sun have met and are shining down positive vibes. This creative sector also deals with falling in love. You might feel ecstatic and euphoric today. Use this energy wisely but, above all, enjoy yourself.

Saturday 30th

Tomorrow, Mercury begins its first retrograde of the year. Take time today under the precision of a Virgo Moon to back up all your devices and double any check travel plans. Be aware that communications could be troublesome over the next few weeks. Always pause before responding.

Sunday 31st

Mercury retrograde begins. You must look at your schedule now and see if there are any jobs outstanding. Tick off your 'to do' list and be steadily productive today. This is a day for tidying and tying up loose ends. Try not to get distracted by fantasies and illusions.

FEBRUARY
. . . .

Monday 1st

February begins with Venus entering your social sector. She will attempt to bring peace and harmony while she is here, so use her energy well. Ego battles may surface as the Sun and Mars are making a difficult connection. This can be useful energy if you need to get things done today.

Tuesday 2nd

Your attention will be outgoing today, and your personal relationships will be in focus. Attempt to balance the needs of everyone where you can. Jupiter will bring you luck and the Sun will energise worn-out connections. Bring lessons learned from the past into this. Be fair and non-judgemental.

Wednesday 3rd

Tact and diplomacy are your best allies today. You may want to delve deeper into a connection but the other may not desire this. Remember that they have boundaries too. Mercury retrograde is at play today and you may see battles of the sexes going on. Resist the urge to control.

Thursday 4th

Have you overstepped a social boundary? An emotional, intense Moon sits opposite Mars and Uranus and tempers may flare. Prepare for the worst with a hard hat on. There may be plenty of fall-outs today, especially if you've taken things too far. You may have to swallow your pride and apologise.

Friday 5th

There is opportunity to transform a bad situation into a good one, today. You will probably have to back-pedal and run over a recent interaction to see what went wrong. If you must excavate a problem, do it with the view to bring out the golden lessons. There will be one or two.

Saturday 6th

Venus meets Saturn today in your social sector. If this is an area where you have caused upset, then rely on Venus to help smooth things over and restore peace. Saturn knows that boundaries were breached and is giving you a nod. First lesson learned. Well done.

Sunday 7th

Today you might look to the past and consider where you may have acted without feeling. You can be annoyed because empathy does not come easily to you. Your home and finances also need a tidy up today. Venus is not happy with the wreckage caused by Mars and Uranus.

Monday 8th

Responsibility is the flavour of the day. You must attempt to correct any wrong-doings and clear your name now. The Moon is in your career sector and your integrity is in the spotlight. Mercury has nothing to say today so you must listen carefully to any advice you are given.

. . . .

Tuesday 9th

You may be feeling sorry for yourself today and walk with your tail between your legs. Authority figures are possibly keeping an eye on you so you must be careful not to step out of line. Neptune helps to dissolve any bad feeling and lets you see clearly where you made mistakes.

Wednesday 10th

The fast-moving Moon passes all the planets in your social sector today. Your mood could swing from buoyant to restricted to joyful. Perhaps a mid-week social gathering will ease this unsettling energy. Mercury retrograde is in a bad connection with Mars so just be aware of the tension.

Thursday 11th

You really must learn to bite your tongue today. If you can do this, the meet up between Venus and Jupiter in your social sector could promise you a lovely time with friends. There is a New Moon today in this sector, this is a great time to draw a line under recent squabbles.

Friday 12th

As the weekend approaches, the atmosphere gets lighter. The Moon makes some nice connections to what are normally difficult planets but you can rest easy. You may have some bright ideas today. You can think outside the box and file this away for another time.

Saturday 13th

Have some time off and drift into the surreal world of the Pisces Moon. This is your dream and spiritual sector; fantasy and illusions happen here. Let the Moon's contact with Neptune wash away any tension. You may sit and contemplate the past and the future today. Mercury retrograde meets Venus so be careful with love connections.

Sunday 14th

Enjoy your Sunday under the dreamy Moon because later this evening you will be back to your wound up and ready-to-go self. You cannot stay in the floaty depths for long. Make sure that what you say in conversations today is true as Mercury meets Jupiter.

Monday 15th

As the Moon is in your sign all day, you may feel more focused on your own needs. There are harmonious connections to your teacher planets today. Note what crosses your path and how you deal with it. Mercury asks that you review recent situations and your part in them.

Tuesday 16th

Someone in the workplace may try to manipulate you or at the very least try to knock your confidence. Deep inside yourself, there should be a good feeling, and this can propel you into the next steps of life with the necessary skills. Some things need to be left behind too.

Wednesday 17th

Today you may expect to surprise yourself. Perhaps buy or create yourself a gift for the home and bring some love to your environment. Saturn might frown upon this, but not if it is something lasting and practical. Do not beat yourself up about being fanciful today, you deserve a small treat.

Thursday 18th

The Sun moves into your dreams sector and will warm up an area you sometimes find uncomfortable to be in. You are emotionally driven to make changes or get things done today. Once again, your home and finances are the subjects of this. You will probably feel guilty about spending money.

Friday 19th

What does your heart want? How are you going to get it? Pleasure-loving Venus needs Mars to bring in the luxury today, but he is not listening. How can you add the Venus touch to your home and finances? Maybe it is time for a room makeover. Energy from Mars will help.

Saturday 20th

Short trips, messages and siblings will be on your mind today. This is a weekend to catch up with relatives, either in person or by phone or message. A trip to a DIY store may be in order as you ruminate over what Venus wants you to do to your home while Mars is there to help.

Sunday 21st

The little trickster planet, Mercury, turns direct today and you can breathe a sigh of relief. If you have upset anyone during this period, you may wish to make amends now. There will be a lot of talking, laughing and maybe even gossip today.

Monday 22nd

As the Moon shifts into your family sector, you will probably notice old habits surfacing. This could be old favourite foods or ways of responding. Note what is truly yours and what was conditioned in you by your family of origin.

Tuesday 23rd

Today is perfect for dreaming freely. Let your inner child out and ask them what their dreams were when you were small. Did you achieve what you wanted? Is there still time to perfect those childhood dreams? Neptune helps you to re-connect to what you once desired for yourself.

Wednesday 24th

You are very good at playing. Be careful that any time you are on show, it is for the right reasons. People love your 'go get 'em' attitude, but make sure it does not get out of hand. You are a leader, so be responsible when you have others following you.

Thursday 25th

Jupiter and Saturn are trying to reach you. Are you too caught up in yourself right now? As Venus leaves your social sector, she asks if there is a balance between your own hobbies and those shared with others. Do a spot check on yourself today.

Friday 26th

Venus now enters your dreams sector where she becomes mermaid-like. She is difficult to catch and will have you alternating between wanting this, then wanting that. The Moon opposite her highlights your indecision. Do you need a retreat? Find some dry land and catch your breath.

Saturday 27th

Today there is a Full Moon in your health and duties sector.
Look at what you have achieved in the last six months in this
area and address what state it's in. Are you as healthy as you
could be? Do you need a detox? Do you need to tighten up your
schedules? Take some time to reflect and assess your needs.

Sunday 28th

There is some wonderful earthy energy for you to make
use of today. Keep your fire burning low and do some yoga,
meditation or even gardening. A brisk walk in nature will do
you the world of good. Home, duties and work are highlighted.

MARCH

· · · · · · · · · · · · · · · · ·

Monday 1st

How are your important relationships? This could be your
lover, your best friend or your boss. When the Moon is in your
opposite sign it is focused on these relationships. Connections
to other planets are favourable today which makes relating
outwards easier for you. Get out and enjoy the company.

Tuesday 2nd

When relationships are balanced and even, those born in Aries
can put all their energy into them. You are perfect at taking
the lead but must ensure that you do not take over. An easy
exchange of give and take is needed for relationships to tick
along nicely. Can you achieve this today?

Wednesday 3rd

The Moon shifts into the intense house of secrets, sex,
death and rebirth. Here is where you like to go deep,
and most of the time you go too deep. Remember others'
boundaries. Keep your fiery energy on a low simmer as
you delve into the mysteries of life. What you find there
might scare or surprise you.

Thursday 4th

Today might see you having difficult conversations. Perhaps
you have got yourself into something and now need to climb
your way out. The deep and intimate waters of a Scorpio Moon
are not meant for you. This is where you need to let another
lead the way or get lost.

Friday 5th

You should see light again and the territory around you seems more familiar. Your internal engine is revved and ready to go on an adventure you feel comfortable with. You may find foreign travel or cultures are on your mind. Maybe it would be best if you went out for a delicious exotic meal instead.

Saturday 6th

You are likely to find that foreign destinations are still on your mind. You might be reminiscing about past travel experiences and yearning for your next trip. This is a good day to plan new travel and you have the backing of travel guide Jupiter and travel agent Mercury. Where would you like to go?

Sunday 7th

Look at what your responsibilities are. Have you achieved success in your career? Do you yearn for more? There is always another mountain to climb. You consider your career path carefully and if you have the energy to do it. Of course you do, you are an Aries, go for it.

Monday 8th

Picture yourself at the top of a mountain looking down. Look across to Neptune in your dream sector and ask him if those dreams are possible or merely fantasy. Right now, you have a chance to bring them to you and ground them into reality for another time.

Tuesday 9th

You feel like you have some control over your future plans.
Great ideas are coming into your consciousness now like
electric shocks. The trouble with your astrological sign is
that you often start things without finishing. Use the energy
from your ruler Mars and learn endurance skills. They will
come in handy.

Wednesday 10th

The Sun sits with Neptune today and the mists clear. Neptune
likes to maintain a shroud of illusion, but he has no chance
today. Something may become obvious to you now. You see a
situation or person for what it really is without all the usual
masks and costumes.

Thursday 11th

You're likely to experience a lot of head chatter today.
Mercury and the Moon are meeting up and emotions and
intellect merge. You will need to sort out the logical from the
emotional. Mars is also in on this and wants you to do this
quickly. The energy will change this evening.

Friday 12th

Be careful now that the Moon has entered your dream sector.
If you did not manage to get a clear head yesterday, you may
feel foggy and confused today. Unfortunately, this can lead to
self-soothing with addictive substances. Use this energy to
write poetry, make messy art or meditate alone.

. . . .

Saturday 13th

The Moon sits with Neptune today, thus emphasising the unclear waters. Old habits die hard, and you will find that you resort back to unhealthy habits. The likes of comfort-eating and alcohol may be used as crutches today. Take control and work with your subconscious. Connect spiritually if you can.

Sunday 14th

Back in your sector of self, the Moon wakes you up and shakes your emotional body back to reality. You should take a good look at future plans. Mars and Saturn lend you self-discipline today. Try to keep a clear head; ignore Venus swimming around with Neptune and trying to lull you back to fantasy.

Monday 15th

Jupiter in your friend zone inflates you with trust and self-confidence. Mercury sits at the very last degree of your social sector asking you to catch up with friends you may have neglected recently. Are there any you can say goodbye to once and for all? Try not to carry dead weight with you now.

Tuesday 16th

You need to start making solid plans for progression. Connections to Pluto are conflicting. The Sun, your ego, wants control and transformation, but the Moon is shying away from it. Make plans but do not act upon anything just yet. Listen to advice from those who know you best.

Wednesday 17th

As the Moon enters your finance and home sector, it can feel more grounded. While here, it will connect to Uranus who can help you think outside the box and problem solve like a genius. You may feel like a schoolchild learning something new but go with it, Saturn has big plans for you.

Thursday 18th

Doing something grounding will help you today. Add some beauty to your home or cook a delicious exotic meal. Feeling comfortable in your home environment is a good base to launch any projects that may take you out of your comfort zone. Enjoy an evening in.

Friday 19th

Getting out and about today will be beneficial. You may have too much going on in your head so share it. Tell people your plans, ask for advice and network where you can. You have the energy to 'do' today. Saturn helps you go as far as you need to right now.

Saturday 20th

Happy Birthday! The Sun enters your sign today and this signals a time where your talents and strengths can really shine. You can see a future path more clearly now and feel emotionally pulled to it. Chatting with close friends and family bring lightness to your day.

Sunday 21st

You may well feel more emotional than usual today as Venus spends her last hours as a mermaid and enters your sign as a warrior goddess. This will give you extra energy, but it will be flavoured with love and compassion. You might find this unsettling to begin with.

Monday 22nd

There is a lot of delicious energy available to you today. You should be sociable and chatty, responsible and spontaneous all in one day. A nurturing Moon allows you to be yourself without judgement. Maternal figures may feature prominently today. Perhaps make it an unofficial Mother's Day.

Tuesday 23rd

The Moon remains in your family sector for most the day. Whilst there, it is also opposite Pluto who needs to transform and control. You may feel that someone is taking your power away, but it is not the case. You are being cared for and need do nothing. Indulge yourself and let it happen.

Wednesday 24th

The lovely Venus is in the heart of the Sun, charging up before emerging fully armoured in your sign. There is some anticipation in the air and there could be some conflict between men and women. Men be warned, Venus is ready for war so choose your battles wisely.

Thursday 25th

You can have a lot of head chatter today as Mercury weighs up old habits and new skills. Self-talk will need to be kind. The Moon in your creative sector just wants to play so perhaps play at being a soldier and have some tactic talks with your inner voice.

Friday 26th

Mars the warrior is sitting on a point called the North Node and is ready to march into the future. For you as Aries, this means that your short trips, communication and siblings sector will get busier. Right now, you should have a health check-up and review your daily and weekly schedule.

Saturday 27th

You'll probably feel the need to do some spring-cleaning today. You can de-clutter like a pro. Look at your items and decide whether they get stored, sold, donated or dumped. This can be done in a regimental way without emotions getting in the way. Mars will like this.

Sunday 28th

As the Moon slips into your sector of 'other', a Full Moon rises. It is asking that you look carefully at what it shows. This will be about balance and harmony in your relationships. Look at the ratio of give and take. If something is off, then it needs to be addressed now.

Monday 29th

Today is like a garden of roses. The Moon makes lovely connections and everything ticks along nicely. You may think that this day of peace is too good to be true, and it is. Enjoy it while it lasts. Today should be a lovely day for romancing and dancing.

Tuesday 30th

The scent of the roses gets heady and intoxicating today. The euphoria is gradually dissolving, and feelings become intense. You think a little deeper now and superficial conversations just do not cut it. You feel like a volcano waiting to blow and do not know why. Jealousy and control issues might surface. Tread carefully.

Wednesday 31st

Today, you want to probe, you want to merge, and you want to know everything about a special someone. You must remember the importance of personal boundaries and only proceed if given permission. The Moon's connection to Jupiter can amplify all of this or it can blow it out of proportion.

APRIL
· · · · · · · · · · · · · · · · · ·

Thursday 1st

Reach out beyond your comfort zones and explore an environment alien to your own. Thoughts may turn to travel and higher education as you want to know what else is out there for you. The Sun in your sign makes you believe that anything is possible if you want it enough.

Friday 2nd

The Moon makes some sweet connections today. This has the effect of sugar-coating the world around you. You are highly optimistic and romantic. This would be a good day to discuss adventures with a loved one or best friend. You may even think about up-cycling old things.

Saturday 3rd

Emotions and words may be at odds today. You must speak your mind and remember to keep them kind, true and helpful. If you cannot do this, then keep your thoughts to yourself. You are outgoing and have an enquiring mind today. Let it wander but stay in control.

Sunday 4th

Mercury enters your sign today. He has completed a circuit of the zodiac and now enters with a new mission for you. His last retrograde was in your social sector and this is where Saturn and Jupiter will hang out this year; perhaps your mission is in this area?

Monday 5th

Today you feel on top of your game in the workplace. Emotionally, you are stable and productive and as the Moon passes through this sector you feel in control of things. This afternoon will bring some connections with friends and wider groups you are involved with. Listen to what is being shared.

Tuesday 6th

There is some tension in the air today which could feel unsettling if you get emotionally attached. Responsibility and restrictions might get too much, and you will need to let off steam. You will probably feel this as a personal assault, but it is not. Lie low, this feeling will soon pass.

Wednesday 7th

Romance is favoured today as the Moon makes helpful connections to Mars and Venus. The Moon also sits with lucky Jupiter so make the most of today's energy. If you are solo, treat yourself to whatever feeds your soul. Reading fantasy novels with a bubble bath is a perfect combination.

Thursday 8th

Today you may feel whimsical and childhood memories fill your mind. You might internally review times gone by and what you have learned from certain episodes in your life. Nostalgia is a trigger for you to re-visit old haunts and make new memories.

Friday 9th

You may be jolted out of your happy place today by your ruler, Mars. He squares off with Neptune who is enjoying reminiscing and you will probably begin to remember the not so nice things from the past. Let it flow and let it go, this is in the past.

Saturday 10th

The Moon jumps into your sign and you feel like yourself again. A reality check gives you the self-discipline you need to enjoy the present time. Take a good look at your schedule and future plans and get back to the action-orientated Aries you are. You are positive and optimistic.

Sunday 11th

Getting things off your chest will be easier today. The Aries Moon sits with Mercury meaning that you are able to say what you mean with great effect. Assertiveness shouldn't be a problem and you may surprise yourself with some deep emotions being voiced. Use this opportunity well.

Monday 12th

A New Moon in your sign is the perfect time to make resolutions that have a good chance of sticking. This Moon sits with Venus adding harmony and compassion to your warrior spirit. Be careful not to throw your weight around or be over-controlling, as Pluto has a say here too.

Tuesday 13th

Money-matters need attention now. You may be tempted to over-spend or impulse buy. If this is something you need to do, make it something for the home environment which you can enjoy for a long time. Saturn is asking that you be responsible with your spending today.

Wednesday 14th

Watch out that you do not get sweet-talked into something that can blow out of proportion today. Venus is at the last degree of your sign and is urging you to seriously consider how you flavour your actions. Always act for the greater good or it will come back to bite you.

Thursday 15th

Your home and finances sector gets a loving boost from Venus as she settles into the sign she rules. Money may come in unexpectedly; your self-esteem should reach a high and you may wish to beautify your home. This is a great day for doing something kind or generous. Communication and chores are easily done today.

Friday 16th

This is a day for making long term plans. You may speak to friends and family who will be eager to listen and share your enthusiasm. Listen to them too as they may have ideas that you have not considered. Network with wider groups such as those on social media.

Saturday 17th

The Moon and Mars meet up and you may feel overly-sensitive and victimised. There will be a lot of discussion and possibly even arguments which you will need to settle by the end of the day. Moon (emotions) and Mercury (mind) are both making a mixed bag of connections.

Sunday 18th

Today is much quieter and you may spend it licking your own wounds or tending to someone else's. Nurturing is the theme of the day. Mercury is in the heat of the Sun and has nothing to say now. Use that compassionate warrior spirit and be firm but fair.

Monday 19th

Both Mercury and the Sun enter your finance and home sector. This adds further tension or energy to this area and all the more reason to get a makeover or treat yourself and friends to a great meal. Indulge yourself and tantalise your senses while the Sun is here.

Tuesday 20th

Someone may try to manipulate you today. There is heavy tension in the air, most likely involving women's issues. You may need to bite your tongue or stand up for someone. Be the hero today and not the manipulator. Say what you mean but say it with love.

Wednesday 21st

Your playful side comes out today, just be mindful to play nice and share your toys. The Moon makes some hard connections whilst in your creative sector which is a warning not to have tantrums with others. You can be childlike and unfiltered in the way you play. Try to be aware of this.

Thursday 22nd

Daily mundane jobs need to be completed before the weekend. What has been neglected and what have you left unfinished? The next couple of days you will need to be thorough and double-check your 'to do lists'. Mars is reminding you that this could involve communication.

Friday 23rd

Time to check in with your health. You are always on the go so much that you cannot see when you are at risk of burn-out. Do not ignore minor health issues. There may well be a surprise love connection today as Venus meets Uranus who likes to be unpredictable.

Saturday 24th

Mercury now also meets Uranus. This is a warning to watch what you say. Mercury is a blabber-mouth and you may say something you shouldn't. Avoid gossip if you can. Neptune the great dissolver has a say today so stay real and watch out for the fakes. Tread mindfully.

Sunday 25th

Today has the potential to be tricky. Venus, the planet of love, and Mercury, the messenger, appear to have a secret rendezvous and this annoys Saturn who is in your social sector. Are you having a party and deliberately missing someone off the guest list? Play carefully with your social circles.

Monday 26th

After a weekend where your attention has been focused on special people in your life, you may now feel a little secretive. If you are attached, then you may notice that intimacy is free-flowing. You may get to know someone on a deeper level while the Moon is in your sex, death and rebirth sector.

Tuesday 27th

A super, sexy, seductive Full Moon occurs today, and you will feel the intensity of it in your one-to-one relationships. However, this could be like getting to the bottom of a volcano only to light the fuse. If you are not careful and sensitive, today could be explosive.

Wednesday 28th

Pluto, the ruler of the Full Moon, goes retrograde today. As he moves slowly you may not feel any effects, but watch out in your career sector. Power and control issues could come out into the open in the next few months. Be on your guard.

Thursday 29th

Where would you like to go to in the world? Your fellow fire sign, Sagittarius, hosts the Moon in your travel sector now. Are you thinking about summer travels or a last-minute impulse trip? Reminiscing about trips in the past can set your itchy feet towards the travel agents today.

Friday 30th

If you have been changing things around your home, then today is the day you may decide that you love it or hate it. Sudden changes of mind and opinion may cause you to be irrational or a genius. Expect the unexpected with appearances and money today.

MAY

. . . .

Saturday 1st

The influence of the Sun and Uranus in your finance sector
may be making things interesting. Impulse buys can be
extravagant. This is also a time when radically changing your
hair or style is favoured. Do yourself a favour and have a treat
which will make you feel shiny and new.

Sunday 2nd

The energy is right for you to ask for anything you want
today. Making changes not only at home but also in your
career are highly favoured now. Venus is at home and has a
list of desires. Dream big and you may see this manifested
sooner than you think.

Monday 3rd

A sociable Moon begins the week. You may have some
innovative ideas you wish to share. Be careful about who you
choose to be a confidant as friendship groups may include a
gossip. A boss or older person will possibly have a lesson for
you today. Take it all in.

Tuesday 4th

Mercury returns home to your communications sector.
Research and data gathering will be easy now. Idle chatter and
mental faculties will be working overtime. Write everything
down and if necessary, lock it away to come back to another
time. You may have too many ideas now.

Wednesday 5th

The Moon meets Jupiter before shifting into your dreams sector. The urge to think big and dream big is encouraged now. At first, you will feel stuck and not sure which direction to pursue. Use that pause; it is there to stop you rushing into something you may regret later. Neither heart nor head have any clarity.

Thursday 6th

Much is happening in the heavens today. You are being asked to turn some ideas on their head and seek out a new perspective before proceeding. Listen to your intuition now. Jupiter is at the final degree of your social sector and asks that you are absolutely sure about certain friendships.

Friday 7th

The Moon dips into your sign today. You should feel energised and eager to get going on new ideas. Recycling or upgrading something to make it more lovable can be a project for you. You could also be doing something positive with your finances or thinking about investing.

Saturday 8th

Demands from family might take you away from your personal plans today. You are so action orientated that when a change of plan interrupts you, it unsettles you. Responsible decisions are made which will have a bearing in the future. Try not to over-spend on luxuries at this time.

Sunday 9th

As the Moon drifts into your finance sector, Venus exits. Love, peace and harmony will be added to your communication style and with Venus here, there is a greater chance of getting what you ask for. Tonight, your emotional needs are best satisfied with a tasty, home-cooked meal.

Monday 10th

A connection from your ruler Mars gives you extra drive today. Making a change such as redecorating the home could keep you up late. Regardless, these unusual working hours are filled with the enthusiasm you need. You may surprise yourself. There is a slim chance that you could be emotionally drained by it.

Tuesday 11th

A New Moon in your home and finance sector arrives just at the right time for your change-making mission. Just check that your plans are not too far-fetched. You may have over-estimated something. This is a good time to talk about your future plans with someone like a professional, bank manager or teacher.

Wednesday 12th

By midday, your mind has more clarity and more solid plans should begin to form. You appreciate your personal limits but also know when and where you can stretch yourself. The Moon and Venus meet up and add a feminine touch which softens the urgency of energy from Mars. Intuition and beauty combine nicely.

Thursday 13th

Jupiter bounces into your dream sector. He will bring good fortune to this area. This influence can also mean that a spiritual teacher will come into your life, but you must use discernment and not be duped by false gurus. Let your head and heart have a little chat today.

Friday 14th

If you are in two minds about something today, put it to one side and come back to it another time. The Moon makes a difficult connection to Neptune, who can cast a mist over your thinking. You may also be asking someone else for their opinion but be objective.

Saturday 15th

Family gatherings can be fun today. Nurturing and nourishment from mothers and female relatives can be a perfect distraction for that busy mind of yours. Listen to feminine wisdom. Home life can provide a cosy atmosphere for a day under the duvet with a good book and comfort foods.

Sunday 16th

You are emotionally driven to be surrounded by your loved ones today. Helpful connections from Mars, Uranus and Neptune can make it a day of pleasant surprises. Empathy for family members runs high. You are all on the same page and the day should run smoothly.

Monday 17th

By midday, the Moon enters your creative sector and you should feel fired up again. Any recent ventures you have explored can now be made solid. You may come up against some opposition in the workplace, but it will not last. This could be your own perceptions and feelings that are slightly hurt.

Tuesday 18th

Are you yearning for a special relationship? You may be reminiscing about lovers past and idealising a future or current one. The Moon in your creative sector also deals with falling in love so today you are a little romantic. Someone you admire may not be accessible to you.

Wednesday 19th

Enjoy some self-expression and laughter. There is nothing wrong with letting your inner child come out and play. This will do you good today. This evening you may be upset by someone in authority; do not let it get to you. Look at why this happened and why it's upset you.

Thursday 20th

How much do you do for others? Are you getting enough time for yourself? If you neglect your health too much, use today to check those aches and pains. Exercise can also help. This is also a good day for sorting a backlog of admin and checking your 'to do' lists.

Friday 21st

The Sun is now in your communications sector and will give you the gift of the gab. Your powers of persuasion and eagle-eyed research will be stronger now. Today you may feel disillusioned by something and will want to speak about it. Now is not the time.

Saturday 22nd

You'll likely have a hard time discerning fact from fiction today. Mercury the messenger is squaring off with Neptune the dissolver. You might feel that you have grasped a concept or idea and then suddenly it is gone again. Don't beat yourself up about it, this is only a few hours of fog.

Sunday 23rd

Saturn goes retrograde today in your social sector. You are
being asked to evaluate your friendship groups. False friends
should fall away now. You must pay particular attention
to your personal boundaries and those of others. You may
have already overstepped the line somewhere and this needs
addressing now.

Monday 24th

Depth and intimacy in important relationships get a boost
from the Scorpio Moon. You may now be exploring secrets
or taboo subjects. The occult will fascinate you. Unravelling
the mysteries of life and death is high on the agenda at these
times. Money matters also require investigation. Something
may come to an end.

Tuesday 25th

You may be feeling the first influence of Saturn retrograde
today. When you are in the seductive depths of the taboo, you
may well cross a boundary which can cause trouble down the
line. Make sure that you and your social groups play safe and
with respect.

Wednesday 26th

A Full Moon in your travel sector can highlight any higher
education or exploration of foreign lands you have done. This
could also be the green light to go ahead with plans of this
kind. You are pulled to look back at the past and let something
go once and for all.

Thursday 27th

If you are after an easy day, then think again. Today's energy is disruptive. Love affairs may be teetering on the edge as empathy is nowhere to be seen. Any illusions or ideals will be exposed, and this could have you questioning your own mind. Some dreams may disappear from view.

Friday 28th

Start at the bottom of the mountain and keep climbing. You wish to see what it is like at the top today. Jupiter lends you some optimism and motivation. Events in the workplace could elevate you to a higher position where that balcony seat awaits you.

Saturday 29th

The old trickster Mercury goes retrograde today. As Venus, the celestial love goddess of love, sits with him, expect to feel this effect in your conversations with a lover. It is essential to communicate well now as Mercury retrogrades through his own sign, and the communication sector of your chart.

Sunday 30th

Try to have a day with your friendship groups. The Moon favours time spent with your tribe but remembers that Mercury can upset things here, too. Get on a bandwagon and rally the troops for a protest or a good cause. You feel for the underdog and care for those less fortunate, put this into action.

Monday 31st

The Moon meets Saturn today. This can mean that your leadership is either questioned or admired. As he too is retrograde, this influence is likely to be a test of your boundaries. Knowing when to push and when to step back in social interactions is essential for keeping the peace. Try to find a balance.

JUNE
. . . .

Tuesday 1st

An emotional overload in your private dreams sector might cause some confusion, as the Moon meets Jupiter there. The Sun meets the point of destiny in your communications sector. Following your dreams and realigning to your soul's purpose should be your focus now. Seeking spiritual nourishment from like-minded souls is the right course.

Wednesday 2nd

Venus answers your calling as she slips into your family sector. Intuition and feminine wisdom will be easier to access. You must nourish your physical body and look at habitual thinking now. Childhood conditioning may no longer serve you; it is time to shed old skin before becoming new. Be unafraid to let go.

Thursday 3rd

Clarity will be difficult to find today; don't try to force it. You might feel a bit lost today as the Moon makes difficult connections. Sit with it and listen to your inner voice, as you should start to see things differently. By evening you will have a better perspective.

Friday 4th

Your own sign and sector of self is visited by the Moon. Activity and emotions are working together now, so follow where they lead. A poor connection from Mercury to Neptune can mean that some form of communication gets lost or misunderstood. Fear not, this will be found again soon.

Saturday 5th

Today will be full of triggers. You may feel victimised and possibly isolated. Your ruler, Mars, is trying to help you push forward but is blocked by control freak Pluto. Spend a Saturday being good to yourself. Take a rest or go for a walk in nature. Nothing will get done today, so try not to put pressure on yourself.

Sunday 6th

Time spent at home will suit you today. The more helpful planets, Jupiter and Venus, are adding some cheer to your home. Decorating, cooking or just buying yourself something bright will make a huge difference. Their influence can also improve your financial situation. You may find some bargains.

Monday 7th

Dreams and future plans are still difficult for you to grasp. Concentrate on other areas for now. An impulse buy could amuse you. Alternatively, someone else may surprise you with a gift. Stay responsible today with your own spending. An innovative idea for the home should come easily.

Tuesday 8th

Planetary energy today is shifting out of the rift slowly. Your natural drive to get things done is coming back. However, you may come across some conflict with a leader or influential person. Someone you have looked up to may disappoint you today. Let it go, this is not as important as you think.

Wednesday 9th

Conversations with close friends and social groups do not
go easy today. Remember that Saturn retrograde is trying to
teach you about personal boundaries. Online groups can be a
wonderful tribe but there is someone there who wishes to rock
the boat. Keep your eyes on the usurpers now.

Thursday 10th

A New Moon in your communication sector also meets
Mercury retrograde today. You can set intentions around
research, learning and speaking, but they may not stick. Be
realistic and make your goals smaller and more achievable.
Aim to connect more physically and vocally with those
closest to you.

Friday 11th

Mercury is in the heart of the Sun today and has nothing to
say. You must listen to anything that comes your way and filter
out the good from the bad. Look for the nugget of wisdom
that you can use in the near future. Mars marches into your
creative sector.

Saturday 12th

You should have extra power to express yourself now. Creative
projects may be started and enjoyed. Family and mothers, in
particular, will feature highly today. There is much love to be
had in a family gathering. This will feed your soul as well as
your stomach. Intuition is strong.

Sunday 13th

Be careful that your ego does not get the better of you today. Your leadership qualities may be challenged, and it is possible that you act out. You can either be emotionally driven to achieve something or be close to erupting. Mothers can help to calm you down.

Monday 14th

Saturn gives you another opportunity to strengthen your boundaries. You will probably feel the need to express what you think about someone. This will not go well. However, the haze of illusion lifts from around a situation and you feel justified in speaking your mind. Revelations will come as no surprise today.

Tuesday 15th

This is a difficult day and there can be a lot of conflict. Mercury is still playing games in your communication sector and friendship groups will be involved. This antsy energy can also be put to good use and several like-minded people together can come up with something innovative today.

Wednesday 16th

Your health is often overlooked. The next couple of days is a good time to get check-ups or resume any fitness regime you may have neglected. Look at how you serve other people and what mundane jobs you do each day. Are you scheduling in some time for yourself?

Thursday 17th

Duty calls but you are also getting demands from your inner life. You are anxious to put some of your plans into action, but other activities are getting in the way. You might find that you are running around doing chores or catching up with emails and messages today. Go with the flow, and find a way to relax this evening if you can.

Friday 18th

Balance is achieved today. Your relationship sector is highlighted over the weekend and you can combine your rest time with someone special. Favourable energy from your ruler helps you to make the day and evening run smoothly. It will be easier to meet your own needs and those of another.

Saturday 19th

Today you should find that the only thing that is out of sync is that perhaps you spend or eat too much. Otherwise, this is a great time to review the ideas you have had recently. This is what Mercury retrograde asks. What can you re-think, re-plan and re-organise? Two heads will be better than one.

Sunday 20th

Interesting conversations with a loved one bring you together in a more intimate way. If you are single, then you can do some soul-searching now. You may find some opposition within yourself to go too deep as you are remembering Saturn's lesson about personal boundaries.

Monday 21st

The Summer Solstice arrives, and you can enjoy the longest day of the year. Jupiter goes retrograde in your dreams sector. This is in the early degrees and he will help you re-think and evaluate your spiritual life. Do not act now, you must assess where spiritual paths might lead you.

Tuesday 22nd

At last, Mercury turns direct and communication, thinking and researching will have more clarity. You may be thinking about studying a course of higher education or going on a long-haul trip. Jupiter loves this, but remember to keep it in the planning stage for now.

Wednesday 23rd

Conflict between home and career or mother and father figures may occur today. There is a battle of wills going on. Someone desires change or control and you may be caught in the middle of this. Good connections to your own ruler and Saturn will help you deal with this the best you can.

Thursday 24th

This afternoon there is a Full Moon in your career sector. Look back at the last six months and see if anything you implemented then has come to fruition now. Your social status and leadership will be highlighted under this Moon, so be sure not to step out of line at work today.

Friday 25th

Yet another of the planets goes retrograde today. Neptune is a slow mover and he has been in your dreams and private sector for several years now. You might be spending much more time alone. There is a danger of unhealthy coping mechanisms or using things such as TV to switch off.

Saturday 26th

Another battle of wills will occur today. Once again, it is the parental or home and work areas that are affected. The Moon sits with Pluto, so it is likely that the patriarchy will win this battle. Join in with a social activity and make your voice heard.

Sunday 27th

You are fired up with rebellious instincts today. You may be breaking some rules or coming very close to starting a revolution. There could be trouble with those in authority. Venus moves into your creative sector and this could mean that a new love is on the horizon.

Monday 28th

You may have been on your soapbox over the weekend. Are you finding it hard to climb down? This is the warrior in you, Mars likes this. The mood changes by evening and you are out of steam. Give yourself some downtime and be alone with your thoughts.

Tuesday 29th

Unusual ideas come to you now. You are able to assess their worth by looking at the past and similar experiences. You muse over what worked before and see if there is a possibility of using it again. Twisting it up and applying it to the current situation seems to work.

Wednesday 30th

The Moon has met up with Neptune retrograde and this may be the first time you feel like being alone. Emotions and communication are not in sync; you'll likely retreat and say nothing. You must process what your heart is telling your head and vice-versa. Listen to your inner voice during this time.

JULY

. . . .

Thursday 1st

The Moon in your sign brings your needs back to making plans. An Aries knows best how to initiate new projects but with most of the planets in retrograde, keep them small for now. Mars wants you to break through some barriers today. Be careful not to be seen as bullying..

Friday 2nd

Better energy helps you to express yourself in a direct but mindful manner. Today you may laugh and let your inner child play. Innocent banter with family members or a lover is just the kind of rough and tumble that Mars likes right now. Have fun with it.

Saturday 3rd

When the Moon enters your finance sector, you need to check your bank balance. A stand-off with Pluto asks you to investigate any money or investments you share with someone else. Try not to spend too much this weekend. Instead, dream of what you would like when circumstances improve.

Sunday 4th

There is no point having a tantrum today, although you may feel like it. You might be feeling guilty about a situation where you lacked control. This has now come back to bite you. Blow off some steam by making messy art or experimental cooking. There is nothing else you can do about it right now.

Monday 5th

Good energy is available for you to take back your self-control. You can make positive steps in ensuring that whatever it was that went wrong can be put right. It is possible that you will have to bring an end to something in order to move forward.

Tuesday 6th

Networking across social groups can give you some interesting new perspectives. However, these are difficult for you to comprehend and put into words. This may make you feel inadequate. Try not to worry; the fog will lift if you stick with it and master the new concepts you have been exposed to recently.

Wednesday 7th

This could be a day for a brand-new love connection. The Moon is making helpful connections to the celestial lovers, Venus and Mars. Both are in your sector concerning falling in love and will meet soon. Just remember the boundary issue as Venus squares off with Saturn.

Thursday 8th

This afternoon may come with a call to go home. You have a need for home comforts and familial love. It is possible that you have a heart to heart with someone. A maternal figure shares her wisdom. Family and friends are both asking for your attention today, but home is where the heart is.

Friday 9th

When in the comfort of your own home or the ancestral home, you feel protected. You are able to speak your mind, even if what you have to say might shock people. This is not a bad thing. Getting something off your chest will help in the long run.

Saturday 10th

A New Moon in your family sector lets you set intentions and goals concerning mothers, your family of birth and the family you have made. Although this Moon sits opposite control freak Pluto, you will consider making changes gently. An empathic time with your kin will pull everyone together.

Sunday 11th

The pull from your social circle is strong today. This is another chance to assess friendships and ask yourself if there is a balance or not. You may need to put someone right on a few things. Try not to be harsh as this may be upsetting. Mercury enters your family sector now.

Monday 12th

Love is on the cards today as Venus and Mars are both touched by the Moon. This is almost telling you to be creative, so write that love poetry or impress a love interest with your creative skills. Eloquence should come easy now, perhaps you have found your muse.

Tuesday 13th

Mars and Venus meet at last. In a fiery sign, this could be a strongly passionate time for you. The Moon moves into your health and duties sector and you have no problem offering yourself up to another to do their bidding. The love bug has bitten you.

Wednesday 14th

The Earth is moving and sparks are flying. Uranus, who is not yet retrograde, is causing a rumble in your finance and home sector. You could be de-cluttering and tidying up in order to entertain someone special. Healthy foods are on the menu today, you may begin a detox programme.

Thursday 15th

Your emotions are adrift and bordering on fantastical thinking. However, the Sun comes along and evaporates the mist, making you see more clearly. You are able to control your feelings and come back to earth. This afternoon you are more balanced and ready to spend time with another.

Friday 16th

Even though your mind and emotions are not really in sync today, you manage to find equilibrium. Shared dreams for the future beckon and you have the utmost respect for another person. Someone you love or greatly admire will open up to you more now that you have shown this.

Saturday 17th

Romance is on the menu once more. You have a balanced approach to getting to know someone and wish to probe deeper. Intimacy is likely this evening, but both the Moon and the Sun are not in a good connection to Pluto. Control issues may be a problem.

Sunday 18th

Jupiter retrograde has now returned to the first degree of your private dreams sector. Merging your dreams with another can be tricky. A Moon opposite Uranus can bring some unrest if you are digging too deep. Be satisfied with having a balanced connection with someone and don't push if they are not ready.

. . . .

Monday 19th

As the Moon shifts, so does your mood. You change the focus
to travel and the wider world. Other philosophies and cultures
interest you now and this these are subjects you will want to
explore with a partner. Jupiter can make these conversations
far-reaching and maybe unrealistic now.

Tuesday 20th

You may be thinking back to past trips and vacations.
Conversations can surprise you and raise new interests. Learn
what you can about what interests you and consider a course
of higher education for a later date. The world may be out
there for you to explore in books or documentaries.

Wednesday 21st

Another great connection from the Moon to Venus and Mars
makes a midweek date or meet-up satisfying. A fiery Moon
arouses passion between lovers. You can light a slow-burning
fire now under your shared interests. Who knows where this
will take you in the future.

Thursday 22nd

Venus moves on from her lover and concerns herself with your
health and duties sector. A little self-love and self-care will be
good for you. If you have neglected a diet or fitness regime,
then now is a good time to re-start it. The Sun moves into
your creative sector and you will be on top form.

Friday 23rd

Taking small steps to get what you want is the way to go. Your tendency to rush right in where your career is concerned will do you no favours. Make a vision board or plan of action to climb the corporate ladder and up-level your status at work. Take things slow and steady; small progress is better than no progress.

Saturday 24th

A Full Moon in Aquarius asks you to look at what you have learned from Jupiter and Saturn this year. Are there still people in your social circle who take too much? Are you still allowing this? Look at what you have achieved and how far you have come.

Sunday 25th

Here is where you might see false friends fall away. There are some control issues going in several areas of your life. Home, work and finances are taking a bashing today. You will be unable to stop yourself speaking your truth to someone now. Male and female energy will clash.

Monday 26th

Take a break and spend some time alone today. You have spent far too much time being of service to others and need to rest and recharge. Emotions can be at a bursting point, so you must use solitude as a crutch and simply switch off the phone and relax.

. . . .

Tuesday 27th

There is a danger today that your alone time can lead you into unknown waters. Neptune hangs with the Moon and reality is hard to grasp. This influence may include unhealthy habits and vices, so be careful. Try watching a favourite TV show or eating ice-cream under the duvet instead.

Wednesday 28th

Planetary shifts can feel like a bump today. The Moon lands in your sign and brings you back down to reality. Jupiter goes back to check out your friendship zone and Mercury chats his way into your creative sector. You will have a hard time keeping up with today's mundane activities.

Thursday 29th

Your ruler now enters your health and duties sector. He asks that you spend more time exercising and looking after yourself. He sits opposite Jupiter before he moves and sees that you have neglected a lot of your obligations and sense of self. Time to spend more time on self-care.

Friday 30th

Take a look at your bank balance today. Joint finances or taxes may need to be reviewed. You have the necessary drive to get all things sorted and tick off a few things on your 'to do' list. Mars gets you moving today in the right direction.

Saturday 31st

Unrest in the family is possible now. Mercury is having his say and sometimes does not know when to be quiet. A family elder or authoritative member is likely to take exception to this and could lay the law down. Take heed, Saturn is your greatest teacher right now and you must toe the line.

AUGUST

. . . .

Sunday 1st

Mercury is quiet now and you must do the same and listen for new information. This may come along as gossip but as Saturn is involved here, you may have to search for it in texts. It may come as a shocking revelation or an ingenious new way of problem-solving. Keep your eyes and mind open.

Monday 2nd

It will seem difficult to have your say today. Emotional needs tend towards sharing and communicating, but you are drained. Teachers may challenge you and make things difficult. Forward motion is at a standstill. Do some meditation to release your pent-up emotions; breathe and let them go.

Tuesday 3rd

Look forwards and imagine a possible future. Where do you see yourself in five years? You feel more positive today. Talking about what you desire will not be taken seriously. Perhaps your dream future does not include someone special. That person will feel this like a kick in the teeth.

Wednesday 4th

Today you cannot do right for doing wrong. You may have run out of ideas and be finding it very difficult to please someone. Irritations can make you retreat and want solitude. Even this does not help, as you are having trouble switching off. Tension bubbles below the surface.

Thursday 5th

Your family can bring comfort now. This is a time when mothers, sisters and other female relatives can offer wisdom you cannot ignore. The Moon makes a good connection to Mars and this wisdom could come in a very direct manner. Women may give you stern but good advice.

Friday 6th

You must get back on track and either apologise or discard your personal dreams. Being in a partnership requires give and take. At the moment, compromise is not easy to reach, and you could easily feel that you are the one doing all the giving. Take time out and process this.

Saturday 7th

Practising eloquent speeches or personal justifications in your head only makes you feel worse. Re-write those words and add some compassion to them. The Moon in your creative sector can help here. Your ego is what is stopping you sorting this situation out. Don't let it win.

Sunday 8th

A New Moon in your creative sector tells you that something may have just ended. This could be a love affair, but not necessarily. However, this also means that there is space now for something new or a fresh start. You may have put your squabbles to one side or decided to walk away.

Monday 9th

Today the Moon enters your health and duties sector. You vow to start the week with all things in place. Loose ends just will not do. You may now share that piece of information that Mercury had you discover. Make sure that there is truth in it.

105

Tuesday 10th

Your drive picks up today. A forgotten exercise or self-care regime may be resumed. A burst of useful energy from Uranus will see you doing things in a new way. There may still be trouble with your love life and those future dreams may come back to tempt you away from real life.

Wednesday 11th

As the Moon meets up with Venus, they have a heart-to-heart. You will receive more of a sense of how two people can serve each other in a love relationship. A gentle nudge from Pluto asks you to transform outdated ways of persuasion into a shared vision.

Thursday 12th

Mercury has now flown into your health and duties sector and will get busy. Daily tasks will be done with more ease. You will have the knack of seeing jobs completed. A lot of earth energy helps you to get grounded and real. You will happily do what is asked of you.

Friday 13th

Try to achieve a balance between making time for others and having time for yourself. This may tug on the heartstrings as relationships are in focus and you just need time alone. You do not want to have to consider another person right now. Have some downtime.

Saturday 14th

Probe deeper and you may just find something worth investigating. The mysteries of life and death are waiting for you to explore. Conversations today may be slightly taboo or bordering on the occult. Remember not to push boundaries too far as Saturn, your teacher, is watching you today.

Sunday 15th

Think about whether you are learning this lesson set by Saturn and Jupiter. When the Moon enters this sector, it makes bad connections with both. It also opposes Uranus, and this signifies that you have gone too far, and something has backfired on you. Gently does it.

Monday 16th

This week starts with a small roller-coaster of emotions. You are more outgoing now, but Mars and Saturn seem to suck in all your energy and put stops on your plans. Venus entering your relationship sector is good news. Expect much more balance, love and harmony while she is here.

Tuesday 17th

Optimism is a welcome change as you go through the day with a smile. You may be under some illusions today, but nobody should really notice. This keeps you in a good mood. Be careful that the illusions are just fancies and that you are not in their grip.

Wednesday 18th

Today you are determined to succeed in all that you do. You may just reach that milestone or solve that problem you have been wrestling with. Work should go well for you. You may have a small niggle with your love life because your attention is required, and work gets in the way.

Thursday 19th

Uranus goes retrograde today in your finance sector. This earth-shaking planet might rock the boat and cause you some money problems. Mercury and Mars together in your health and duties sector urge you to check your bank accounts and make sure all is in order. This influence may cause indigestion too.

Friday 20th

The weekend begins with a struggle. You may be the centre of attention in some circles but not all. Throwing your weight around with people you may not know very well will cause you to lose face. Nobody likes a show-off. Offer valid opinions and not judgements.

Saturday 21st

Your social circle gets another hit. You could be upsetting a lot of people here. On the other hand, the link to Uranus may also mean that you are joining in political activist marches or protests. Another view of this is that together with others you come up with something unique.

Sunday 22nd

A Full Moon at the final degree of your social sector asks you to take a very good look at those you connect with. When the Moon shifts this afternoon, the energy is softer, and you have far more empathy for your tribe. You desire to merge with the collective.

Monday 23rd

You feel a bit directionless today and this will make you irritated. Women save the day today; female teachers will share their wisdom. Listen to what they have to say as this could be a valuable lesson. It could concern your relationships and social groups. Aim for balance here.

Tuesday 24th

Aim to sort out fact from fiction today. There will be a lot of fog around something you need to absorb. Headaches are likely as your brain is taxed and this will not help. Attending to the daily tasks will help you to focus more on the tangible and less on the ethereal.

Wednesday 25th

The Moon makes its monthly visit to your sign but now opposes Venus. You could be selfish and disregard people who are important to you. The brain fog continues to prevent you from getting clarity. Be ready to take a break and revisit issues at another time.

Thursday 26th

Take a look at any monies or investments you have with another person or company. The law may be involved, as Jupiter has a say today. This is not likely to be a bad thing but you should ensure that you are on the right side. Trying to start something new is not possible now.

Friday 27th

Your personal finances could tie up your time now. Spending on something for the home will give you pleasure but will affect your bank balance in a negative way. Social events could be costly over the weekend, perhaps it is best to decline invitations that will stretch your wallet.

Saturday 28th

A fine dining or spa experience could be just what the doctor ordered. You may overspend this weekend but do so on something memorable. You want to let off some steam and a bit of retail therapy appeals to you. Love and romance are highlighted for this evening.

Sunday 29th

You are extra chatty today. Vocalising your dreams is the first step to implementing them. Remain in control of what you say and to whom. All chores get done and there is time to relax at the end of the day. Switch off with a good book or TV show.

Monday 30th

Mercury enters your relationship sector. You can now find important people, lovers or business partners who are totally on your wave-length. Conversation and exchanging ideas should come easily now. This is good news in a love relationship where you are getting to know someone better. Remember to respect their boundaries.

Tuesday 31st

You may have pushed yourself in something such as exercise. Perhaps you do not feel like exercising at all. Alone time under the duvet with ice-cream and a book is where you would rather be. You have duties to attend to; get these done first and then relax.

SEPTEMBER

· · · · · · · · · · · · · · · · ·

Wednesday 1st

Your family environment serves as a haven today. Emotions and mind are not in sync. It is difficult for you to focus on outside matters. Important relationships have no chance of understanding until you have nourished yourself. Have as much home time as you need, this will do you good.

Thursday 2nd

If you do not get your own needs met today, there could be trouble. Lovers may want your attention, but they must understand that right now you are taking care of yourself. Let them know that your downtime will only make your time together more special. Try not to self-medicate now.

Friday 3rd

There are power struggles in your career sector today. A boss or authority figure is not your favourite person. This afternoon you are more able to express yourself and getting your views heard will appease this person. Credit is due to you for not acting out.

Saturday 4th

You could be still seething over a recent injustice. Talking to someone helps but there are also people who will oppose you today and keep your bad mood going. Be the kind warrior, be forceful and direct but do it with kindness. Turn your angst into poetry or messy art.

Sunday 5th

A nice connection from the Moon to Venus will help to smooth over the frazzled edges of late. Social invitations come to you, but it is best that you decline or defer for another time. You can talk to a trusted friend who will offer good advice. Learn from this.

Monday 6th

The Moon helps you to start the week attending to routine duties. Just getting your head down and getting on with small tasks will help. A niggle from a lover may spoil the day. You are in no mood to be manipulated, even if it is wrapped up in sweetness and light.

Tuesday 7th

A new Moon in your health and duties sector gives you an opportunity for introspection. Why do you do what you do? Who are you serving? What bad habits can you lose now? This is a great time to start a fitness regime. You also see through illusions now. Try to be proactive.

Wednesday 8th

Midweek acts as a pivot on which you find a balance between your own needs and another's. You have more time to spend with a lover or partner. Catching up with a friend or two is also possible. Do not spread yourself too thin or you will be drained again.

Thursday 9th

The Moon meets Mercury today and it is likely that a heart-to-heart with a lover or a productive business meeting will occur. A small battle of wills reminds you about personal boundaries but this time it is another who has overstepped them. You're able to put them gently in their place.

Friday 10th

Make time for a sexy weekend. The Moon meets up with Venus and they share their desires. They both move into your intimacy sector today, so expect to be sharing the weekend with a lover. Venus in this house is the seductress, the temptress or the dominatrix.

Saturday 11th

Be careful that your weekend activities do not result in power games being played. One person could be wearing a mask and being passive-aggressive. You will have to lay the law down on someone who is coming on too strong. This could be someone in the workplace or a friendship group.

Sunday 12th

This morning may be troublesome with someone who believes that they are an authority. This could be in your social media groups. You can get to the bottom of this easily and expose them. Saturn is pleased with you today and you have extra points for clearing out rubbish.

Monday 13th

An outgoing Moon brings you back to thinking about your travel wishes. You find that you can only dream about this at the moment as the finances and free time are not available to you. A course of education can satisfy this desire. Sign up now, the time is right.

Tuesday 14th

The Sun sits opposite Neptune in your dreams sector. This has the effect of burning off any idealistic thinking you may have had. Fantasies remain just that, but you are now able to understand why. Not all things are possible. You'll feel a little disgruntled by this.

113

Wednesday 15th

Discussions with a partner may not go so well today. There may be some distasteful revelations which alter the way you think about someone. Your ruler moves into your relationship sector heralding a time of high energy and sex drive, or violence and conflict. Which will it be?

Thursday 16th

Your self-control is good today. You may find that your thoughts want to drift off and take you away from the job, but you resist and manage to pull back every time. An early weekend social event is possible. This could be that you meet friends at an exercise class.

Friday 17th

Venus is not getting her own way today which means that you might neglect or cancel a date with your lover. Be very careful that jealousy and suspicion do not make your actions any larger than they need to be. Be firm but kind with people who push your buttons.

Saturday 18th

Dealings with people who are larger than life surface today. Of course, this could always be you and your ego getting inflated. Spiritual teachers may not be all that they seem. Preached messages may be intoxicating and attract you, but they may actually turn out to be poisonous. Be mindful.

Sunday 19th

The Moon is in your dreams sector and you swim this way and that. Nothing is tangible today and you cannot grasp concepts very well. Venus is continuing to seduce you into taboo or occult mysteries. Strange ideas and thoughts will occupy your Sunday afternoon. Try to use today to get more grounded.

Monday 20th

A Full Moon in your dreams sector will show how you have been changing your perspective on a lot of ethereal topics. You may be on a spiritual path now, one that you had not considered before. Spending time alone, strengthening boundaries and making better connections is good for you.

Tuesday 21st

You sense that the Moon has come into your sign because you have more energy. Your ruler, Mars, is right opposite and lends forward thinking and action to an otherwise irrational Moon. Your internal engine is revving up and you feel good. Positivity fills you and the road ahead is clear now.

Wednesday 22nd

Today marks the Autumn Equinox and day and night are equal lengths. Before tipping into the darker months, pause and reflect. You feel the pull of sexy Venus and a midweek date night is on the cards. Do not probe too deep getting to know someone's secrets.

Thursday 23rd

With the Sun now in your relationship sector, you should feel some warmth and illumination. However, there is still some difficulty with casual conversation. One of you is not opening up as much. With Venus opposing Uranus, there may be a lover's tiff. Remember to give and take.

Friday 24th

The best thing to do this weekend is to treat yourself to a little luxury. You may feel more needy than usual but prefer to appease this with food, wine and gifts to yourself. There is a possibility that you could overspend now or have a tantrum if opposed.

Saturday 25th

Your senses are in overdrive today. Watch out with unhealthy vices, crutches and habits, as you do not need these in order to feel good. There may be some passive-aggressive behaviour going on, which is a very good reason to keep your wits about you. Mars energy is high today.

Sunday 26th

Watch out, it is Mercury retrograde time again. He goes back over the same ground in your relationship sector. Both Sun and Moon contact the point of destiny today and you consider where your future is headed and what skills and life lessons you wish to learn.

Monday 27th

Conversations can be fun today with much laughter. A connection to Neptune asks that you take care to see through people who come across as inspirational. You could change your mind very quickly about them. Then again, you could change it back twice as quick. You are fickle today.

Tuesday 28th

No more fun conversations. Mercury retrograde is already causing chaos. Emotionally you do not know what you need today and could be very misunderstood. Fortunately, by late afternoon, the Moon shifts into your family sector and you know best how to get those needs met now.

Wednesday 29th

Filling up the fridge with comfort foods and snacks will alleviate any yearning for security. However, it is real people, particularly mother figures, who nurture you the best today. You feel nourished and cared for in the presence of strong females. Intuition is strong today so listen to it.

Thursday 30th

A lot of water energy makes this an emotional day. This can weigh heavy on a fire sign like you. Lover, mothers and your spiritual life are all connected today, and feelings can overflow. You could be manipulated by seductive women and sweet-talkers now. Important relationships must be handled with care.

OCTOBER

. . . .

Friday 1st

On the whole, you feel well balanced and outgoing. Optimism fills you and you can express your desires to a loved one. This may not be the same at work, pesky Mercury is squaring off with Pluto and causing trouble in the workplace with close acquaintances. Stick to the rules today.

Saturday 2nd

If you feel compelled to tell someone a secret, beware of who you choose to share it with. Sexy Venus in a sector which deals with taboo can manipulate you into sharing more than you intended. You may be digging a big hole which will be troublesome to climb out of.

Sunday 3rd

Getting ready for Monday by checking your 'to do' list is the flavour of the day. There may be a list of Sunday chores needing your attention. Friends and lovers want your attention, but there is no time today. Do the right thing and see to the daily grind.

Monday 4th

The week starts on a good foot and you are feeling serious and work orientated. You have no time for daydreams or spiritual stuff today. Surprise yourself and expend some nervous energy at the gym or work flat out on a project. Nothing will go unchecked today.

Tuesday 5th

Lovely energy comes in this afternoon and you let yourself relax. A lover may seduce you but in a gentle way. There is a great balance between you and a partner. You are looking after yourself better these days. Time spent with another or spoiling yourself is time well spent.

Wednesday 6th

Today there is a New Moon in your relationship sector. This will meet up with your ruler, Mars, making you activate something new in relating. You can be quite assertive now. Later, the Moon meets Mercury retrograde in the same sector; make sure everyone is on the same page to avoid upsets with important people.

Thursday 7th

Pluto is now direct, and you will feel less like people are coaxing you out of your comfort zone. Venus enters your travel sector and will help you taste the delights of foreign lands. Ideas for studying different cultures or religions will come to you. This is worth exploring.

Friday 8th

Your ego and energy are on fire right now. This weekend you will be filled with adrenalin and possibly initiate several projects at once. You must play by the rules and not go expecting too much from someone. They may not have the same goals as you.

119

. . . .

Saturday 9th

Make a fluid agenda for the day. The planetary action is extreme. Your love life may be disrupted or totally silent. Mercury is speaking to Mars and they both want action they are not going to get. This has you looking back and yearning for the past when, allegedly, life was easier.

Sunday 10th

Saturn now goes direct too. Any obstructions you may have felt in your social circle will ease off and you will see them as important lessons. Other connections to the Moon are easy, giving you a relatively co-operative time with a lover or other special person.

Monday 11th

You are outgoing and optimistic as you start the week. Travel plans have been on your mind, but you are yet to make anything concrete. This distracts you from your work somewhat but does not interfere with it. Keep up that good cheer. As a fire sign, it suits you.

Tuesday 12th

Ideas flow and your neural pathways light up constantly. You should impress all your work colleagues with efficiency today. It will be easy to climb that corporate ladder with all eyes watching. Performing under pressure seems like a walk in the park. Just don't let it go to your head.

Wednesday 13th

Nice energy and your good mood continue to make this week fly by. You may have to bring something to a natural end or scrub it clean and make it new. Allow yourself to dream a little now and get out the travel brochures. There could be an educational trip waiting for you.

Thursday 14th

The Moon drifts into your social sector and meets with newly direct Saturn. You get the first pat on your back for discerning false friends from true ones. A little niggle in your social groups can muddy the water but you should now know how to deal with this graciously.

Friday 15th

Are you ready for the weekend? Once again, you fill with joy and look forward to time with friends. This could be with online groups, too. Your leadership qualities may be called on now and this makes you feel important. Watch that ego, you don't need it stroked.

Saturday 16th

Today, if you do not feel like being sociable, you should stay home and switch off. You could have a crisis of conscience now and decide that you need to spend more time on spiritual matters. Yoga and meditation attract you and finding a spiritual tribe means more to you now.

Sunday 17th

Jupiter joins the party and turns direct in your social sector. This is a great help as he is associated with spiritual teachers and the search for truth. You spend time in meditation or simply thinking about things in a brand-new way. Prepare for a new download.

Monday 18th

Mercury also goes direct in your relationship sector. You feel this shift as it is a more personal one. You now need to talk directly to lovers or important partners. The Moon in your sign helps you to be assertive and kind. Now is the time to initiate new projects.

Tuesday 19th

The planets are all saying that you are good to go. Travel and spiritual matters can be communicated now. Say what is in your heart with full expression. Your ruler gets a good luck charm for you from lucky Jupiter. Get a game plan and make a start.

Wednesday 20th

You might feel resistant or hesitant to put your plans in action today. This will pass quickly. A Full Moon in your sign is all the permission you need. Look back at the last six months at how your intentions have manifested. Have the planetary retrogrades taught you something valuable?

Thursday 21st

The weekend has not begun yet, but you will consider an evening out. Is this because you are avoiding a task that needs doing? You act like a child today if you cannot get your own way. Do your chores and the reward will be much sweeter.

Friday 22nd

Lovers may cause tension as their needs clash with your career priorities. Business partners or people you have joint financial interests with also take up much of your time. You must bring closure to any ties you have with another that are no longer valid or useful. This may upset someone close to you.

Saturday 23rd

The Sun now enters your intimacy sector. This also deals with joint finances and closures, thus amplifying the energy from yesterday. The Moon shifts into your communication sector. Mercury's sign also deals with merchants, so perhaps it's time to make an appointment with the bank. Look at all your options carefully.

Sunday 24th

The urge to spend money on travel is strong today. Venus wants to experience and delight in the exotic. You must control this until money, which Venus also rules, is balanced or accessible. Mercury has your mind doing overtime and you feel that the weekend has gone by without fun.

Monday 25th

You begin the week with a good work ethic. Dreams and plans are put to one side and concentration is strong. Your energy is on top form and can help bring important people into alignment with you. Bosses or influential people in your social groups will notice this.

Tuesday 26th

When you are shopping, be sure to add comfort foods or favourite meals to your menus. Coming home to these dinners will bring you inner security this week without the need for others. Enjoy making yourself feel good and dream about your plans just a little.

Wednesday 27th

Although home is a comfort right now, you may find some opposition from people who want your attention. The work place may be taxing you and it is more difficult to switch off in the evenings. You are still having a background commentary from Venus who wants to explore foreign lands.

Thursday 28th

Tension builds from a lover or business partner. Fortunately, you are able to express yourself well today and smooth things over. A mini personal crisis enters your head in the late hours, this could be something you have neglected at work or a person in authority who has upset you.

Friday 29th

Watch that your direct way of communicating does not get you into trouble today. You say what is on your mind very easily, but it comes out unfiltered. A careless remark or comment can cause a volcano to erupt. Is this your volcano? This will be quickly resolved before the weekend.

Saturday 30th

Your ruler, Mars, moves into the other sign he rules. This is your intimacy sector and so this weekend is great for getting to know someone deeper. This could be a sexy time or a time where arguments with a lover are more likely. Remember not to probe too deeply.

Sunday 31st

A calmer Sunday has you tidying up, de-cluttering and checking in with your health. Jobs on your 'to do' list are more easily completed, bringing satisfaction. You enjoy the thought of getting things in order before the working week begins again. There may even be time to go to the gym today.

NOVEMBER
· · · · · · · · · · · · · · · ·

Monday 1st

Ideas flood into your head today. There is no time for clouded thinking or emotion, it is all about clarity and vision. Relations with lovers or partners are favoured under the influence of Mercury and good luck planet, Jupiter. Conversations are uplifting and optimistic.

Tuesday 2nd

Mercury is squaring off with Pluto today. This could mean that lovers and co-workers clash now. Both require your attention. A balancing Moon in your relationship sector will help you to deal with this in a manner that suits all. Try not to be manipulated.

Wednesday 3rd

An emotional heart-to-heart with someone close will help to prevent any subtle power games going on. You must be firm but fair to avoid any misunderstandings. You have lucky Jupiter on your side so use him well. Look for the truth, the justice and the balance in any conflict.

Thursday 4th

The Moon slips into your intimacy sector. Sex, death, rebirth and shared finances will be up for review. A New Moon today in this sector urges the need to make intentions and goals in these areas. Aggression and restriction may block your path forward for now. Stick with it, this will soon ease.

Friday 5th

Be careful today, exposure is the theme. Fools, liars and cheats are in the firing line, so make sure you are not one of them. Mercury and Venus both shift signs. He goes to the underworld of your psyche and she becomes the lady boss. Fairness and equality in the workplace will be investigated.

Saturday 6th

Easy energy gives you a quiet Saturday. Private investigations are not urgent but occupy your mind over the weekend. This could simply be that you have found something you wish to learn about and now have the time to study. Skills learned in the past are useful now.

Sunday 7th

Your dream life seems to have gone askew lately. Tangible duties and experiences seem more important. This might niggle you somewhat and compel you to rethink your future travel plans. Do not fear, the impulse to create a vision in your mind will return.

Monday 8th

Your obligations and responsibilities take up your mind space as the working week begins. Your energy is on top form. Communication, compassion and assertiveness all go a long way to make this a day you are praised for your efficiency at work. Enjoy this energy, you deserve it.

Tuesday 9th

You need to look at something from a different perspective today. Either your opinion or the thing itself needs to be transformed. There is gold to be found here but the lead is all that is showing. Do some investigating and find the worth in something you are almost ready to discard.

Wednesday 10th

Very heavy energy from the Moon, Mercury and Mars makes this quite an intense day. Heated discussions are very likely. Mars and Mercury are both mining for information in your intimacy sector so this will involve lovers. Saturn makes his presence very obvious and reminds you to respect boundaries.

Thursday 11th

Social groups including activism can create hostility today. Protest marches and petitions can come up against the law and stir up some trouble. Closer to home, you may fall out with friends who have high opinions of themselves. A day of unrest where anything could happen and probably will.

Friday 12th

Retreat for the weekend. The Moon has landed in your dreams sector and you long to be alone with your thoughts and personal visions. Venus connects nicely to the Moon lending you beauty, balance and harmony. Your thoughts can go quite deep today; the mysteries of life fascinate you.

Saturday 13th

Meditation or yoga are the best things you can do today. Enjoy peace and stillness and try to clear your mind. If this is not possible, surrender to whatever comes to you and see where it leads. You may surprise yourself as something from your unconscious comes up for healing.

Sunday 14th

Are you receiving messages from the divine? You may think it is a creation of your own mind but nevertheless, it is something you can work with. Pluto asks that you change something for the better. By afternoon, you are feeling yourself again as the Moon enters your sign.

Monday 15th

You will feel as if nothing is going right for you today. The two luck bringing planets, Venus and Jupiter, are squaring off with Moon and Sun. Ego and emotions must be put to one side or you will feel this intensely. Saturn is watching to see how far you can go without breaking.

Tuesday 16th

An altercation at work may prove challenging but you will come off the winner. Stay strong and use your powers of persuasion. Do not let your emotions get the better of you. Changes will be made but they will be worth it and will bring you good fortune.

Wednesday 17th

The Moon moves into your money sector today and you will be looking at how you value almost everything in your life. Consider how authority figures have shaped you this year. What strengths have you gained. Electrically charged energy around finances get things moving or changing today.

Thursday 18th

Neptune sees to it that your mind and emotions both have attachments that need dissolving. Uranus gets in on the act too by sitting with the Moon in your money sector. More shake-ups regarding money and value are likely now. Do not resist, this is a necessary change.

Friday 19th

A Full Moon in your money sector illuminates just how much things have changed here. You may have invested with another and can now see if it was worth it. This afternoon, communications with siblings may offer good advice and encouragement. A nice surprise awaits you as a reward.

Saturday 20th

Everybody wants to give you their opinion today. There are nuggets of wisdom to be had if you discern wisely. Otherwise, the mental chatter can be too much for you and overwhelm your mind. Friends mean well but today it is best to say thank you and retreat in order to process all that information.

Sunday 21st

Your brain feels full of fog today. There is nothing you can do to gain clarity, and this frustrates you. Use the rest of the weekend to switch off with meditation, a walk in nature or a good book. You will not see clearly until the Moon passes its connection to Neptune.

Monday 22nd

Visits to family or a maternal figure can soothe your over-wrought brain today. Go to someone where you can be yourself and be nurtured. A loving connection between Venus and Mars means that work and passion combine well. The Sun now warms up your travel sector and revitalises that urge.

Tuesday 23rd

You feel that you would like to spend more time in the comfort of your own home or that of a parent's today. Like a child, you resist grown up life and its responsibilities. This is OK, just do not let it be seen in the workplace.

Wednesday 24th

Mercury is done investigating the depths of your psyche and has now left for foreign lands. Anything he may have triggered now needs to be healed. You may have some conflict with an authority figure in the workplace today. Speak your truth with courage, compassion and kindness for all.

Thursday 25th

Is there someone in your social circle whom you greatly admire? Today they may challenge you to think about personal boundaries once again. Thoughts about skills learned in the past come up, maybe there is now a need for them to be put to good use.

Friday 26th

Another leader or authority figure challenges you. Your own leadership skills are questioned, and you have to justify yourself. If you are in any way emotional about this, you will not get very far. You must make yourself seen and heard without having a tantrum.

Saturday 27th

Today you must get things in order. A tidy office or home will help you think more clearly. This is a time to wind things down or think about completing projects already started. What is hanging around that is no longer needed or not doing you any good?

Sunday 28th

Neptune wants to whisk you away to fantasy land, but you are advised not to go there. The best thing to do with this energy is to have a scented salt bath. Adding bad habits and unhealthy coping mechanisms to the mix will make you too far to reach when you're needed. Try to stay grounded.

Monday 29th

Mercury is in the heat of the Sun and has nothing to say, your job is to listen. Your ruler is in connection to Neptune and is also urging you to take action with your dreams. This is conflicting energy, so listen for messages and directions showing whether to act or be still.

Tuesday 30th

Today you feel more outgoing and wish to connect with a partner. Dreams and boundaries can be merged now, making today great for romantic shared visions. Work may be a stick in the mud, but this can be avoided or dealt with easily. Plan those future trips now.

DECEMBER
. . . .

Wednesday 1st

Neptune turns direct today and any illusions you have harboured in recent months should dissolve. Clear sighted dreams will now be more realistically attainable. You have an urge to delve deep and luck will be on your side. Great discoveries are possible now.

Thursday 2nd

Consider your limits and stretch yourself today. This may cause you discomfort but will help you grow. Remember what a caterpillar must go through to become a butterfly. A nice connection between the Moon and Venus helps make the workplace happy today; there will be more harmony between the workers and those in charge.

Friday 3rd

A boost of energy from your ruler, Mars, makes you more outgoing and extroverted. Watch that this does not rattle someone in charge. Keep your drive low key but do not stifle it. Today you need to spread your wings and look over the horizon.

Saturday 4th

A New Moon in your travel sector helps you to put vacation or higher education plans into action. Seek information and research adventures you wish to take. You will know if this is realistic or not, but either way you can still dream. Make an action plan of small achievable goals.

Sunday 5th

You are responsible and considerate today. Your mind is brought back to considering how to climb the mountain of your vision. It may seem huge at the moment. Keep your head out of the clouds until you are at the summit and the view makes you feel proud. You can do this.

Monday 6th

All the outer planets are connecting to the Moon in your career sector today. The helpful connections help you to see the bigger picture and where your seemingly small part in it is. Change the world, or just yourself one step at a time. You will surpass yourself.

Tuesday 7th

This morning the Moon meets up with the planet of permanent change and will aid you in bringing closure to something no longer useful. By afternoon, your vision is still very much in your line of sight. You may seek advice from close friends or online interest groups to spur you on.

Wednesday 8th

A friendly teacher or inspirational person is worth talking to, today. You might butt heads in a radical conversation, but this is meant to get you thinking. Discussing subjects that are outside the box will get your motor running ready for the big journey ahead of you.

Thursday 9th

Any conflict today is likely to be blown out of proportion. Alternatively, your energy could be so great that you burn the candle at both ends or run a marathon. Try to slow down in the afternoon and get ready for a dreamy weekend.

Friday 10th

You may connect with others who are spiritual today. Your mood is changeable, and you are open to new ideas. If yoga or meditation is your thing, then time spent on these will be beneficial. Empathy is strong and friends may seek you out to cry on your shoulders. Allow them the space.

Saturday 11th

A Saturday retreat with a good book or a group of like-minded people will calm you today. Dreams and visions take you to your own inner world and get you looking at things from a different perspective. Listen to your inner voice while there, what is it saying?

Sunday 12th

Venus and Pluto meet up today in your career sector. This can be manipulative energy and you will need to watch out amongst certain people. It can also be that you make a big change which will bring great pleasure. Another aspect is that a love affair could end or be transformed.

Monday 13th

Mercury now enters your career sector. He deals with trade and commerce so use him wisely while he is here. Business talks will be more frequent and deals can be signed. Mars also shifts, marching into your travel sector and stepping up his game with your plans to explore new territory.

Tuesday 14th

You may have trouble with a female co-worker or feel belittled today. A lady boss or woman in authority, possibly even a mother-figure, will try to undermine your efforts. Use your words kindly today, keep your integrity and do not fall to backstabbing or gossip.

Wednesday 15th

Boundaries get breached today. They may be yours or another's and this will cause unrest. You might feel emotionally drained and rely on conditioning and old habits to get you through the day. This will pass quickly, so don't dwell on it – it's not worth it.

Thursday 16th

Today has a better energy attached. Harmony is restored in the workplace and any changes made are easily implemented. This is a change for the better as you will see when you think about it. Don't let someone with an overinflated ego take over any of your social group activities.

Friday 17th

There is a lot you need to communicate or take time to process today. This may make you irritated as it's probably not what you want to be doing. You are revved up for the weekend but there are jobs that need completion and people to contact before you can relax.

Saturday 18th

Venus goes retrograde today. This is a period of time where love affairs can end or someone from you past will reappear. To help make this better for you, set your mind to work and your responsibilities. Duty, and whatever pays the bills, comes first.

Sunday 19th

Today there is a Full Moon in your communications sector.
Along with Venus newly in retrograde, this will highlight
how you think, speak and listen to people in authority. You
may have been in two minds about a situation or person,
but now you will receive clarification. This could also bring
some relief.

Monday 20th

The Moon is now in your family sector and you have the need
to hunker down and surround yourself with the familiar and
comfortable. You are in the mindset for a working week and
this can cause some tension in the workplace. Use this time to
process new ideas.

Tuesday 21st

The Winter Solstice is here, and the shortest day may be
a little depressing. Keep allowing yourself to feel comforted
by nurturing people and eating nourishing foods. A festive
family meal will appease those needs. The winter ahead of
you does not need to be long and dark; it can be warm
and cosy.

Wednesday 22nd

Today you are able to express yourself well. Stand in the
limelight and appreciate the glow. You might rub someone up
the wrong way, but this is not your fault. You have fiery energy
and need to burn it off today. Be creative and loving, and let
your inner child play.

Thursday 23rd

Jupiter sits at the final degree of your social sector. His year-long stay here has shown you who are true friends and gurus, and you may have found your soul group. This critical degree asks that you make sure all is in order in this area before he moves on.

Friday 24th

This is a busy time for all, and the planets are showing this. Go at your own pace and get the chores done. You feel a duty to help and do more than your fair share today. There will be power struggles and tension. Take the pressure off elders in the family.

Saturday 25th

Christmas is here and brings nice surprises but also the usual annoyances. You may not have time to relax and enjoy the day. The first effect of Venus retrograde will be evident today with her meet up with Pluto. This can be controlling or transforming.

Sunday 26th

There is softer energy today after yesterday's rush. You are more likely to kick back and put your feet up. Relationships go well and conversations will range from loving responsibility to the mildly ridiculous. Have fun with family games and silliness. Laughing and dreaming go hand in hand today.

Monday 27th

A balancing Moon energy sees that you get your own needs met while also seeing to the needs of others. Important people such as partners appreciate your efforts today. Much can get done in good spirits. You remember personal boundaries, which is important while Venus is in retrograde.

Tuesday 28th

The energy shifts and makes for a day of misunderstandings. A bossy person may upset you today. It might be a good idea to step way from it all and have some alone time. You will be deep in thought in the evening as bigger life issues take you away from the mundane and small talk.

Wednesday 29th

Jupiter, the luck-bringer steps into your sector of dreams and spirituality. As a guru or preacher figure you will notice that you reach out more to connect with the divine in the next year. You will feel this as a big push, and it will unsettle you.

Thursday 30th

Mercury meets Pluto today and they talk about the gold hidden in your psyche. Something inside you is ready to come up for healing now. You have what it takes to do some introspection and follow the necessary paths to do your soul work. Well done, you can do this.

Friday 31st

On the last day of 2021, you look back at what worked and what did not. You are emotionally driven towards your goals now. There is an attachment to these which you do not want to let go of. Enjoy any get-togethers tonight, you will bring fun to the party.

Aries

....

PEOPLE WHO SHARE
YOUR SIGN

PEOPLE WHO SHARE YOUR SIGN

. . . .

History books and social media feeds are full of pioneering Arians who have blazed the way for decades. From several American Presidents, to famous footballers, Olympians, politicians, activists, actors and YouTube sensations, discover below which of these trendsetters share your exact birthday and see if you can spot the similarities.

21st March

Rochelle Humes (1989), Anna Todd (1989), Ronaldinho (1980), Deryck Whibley (1980), Matthew Broderick (1962), Rosie O'Donnell (1962), Gary Oldman (1958)

22nd March

Nick Robinson (1995), Tyler Oakley (1989), Allison Stokke (1989), Gaz Beadle (1988), Reese Witherspoon (1976), Andrew Lloyd Webber (1948), William Shatner (1931)

23rd March

Kyrie Irving (1992), Vanessa Morgan (1992), Mo Farah (1983), Russell Howard (1980), Perez Hilton (1978), Keri Russell (1976), Chaka Khan (1953), Joan Crawford (1905)

24th March

Jim Parsons (1973), Chris Bosh (1984), Peyton Manning (1976), Alyson Hannigan (1974), Tommy Hilfiger (1951), Alan Sugar (1947), Mary Berry (1935), Harry Houdini (1874)

25th March

Justin Prentice (1994), Big Sean (1988), Danica Patrick (1982), Casey Neistat (1981), Sarah Jessica Parker (1965), Elton John (1947), Aretha Franklin (1942), Gloria Steinem (1934)

26th March

Louise Thompson (1990), Von Miller (1989), Keira Knightley (1985), Lesley Mann (1972), Stephen Tyler (1948), Diana Ross (1944), Leonard Nimoy (1931), Guccio Gucci (1881), Robert Frost (1874)

27th March

Jessie J (1988), Manuel Neuer (1986), Fergie (1975), Kendra Scott (1974), Nathan Fillion (1971), Mariah Carey (1970), Quentin Tarantino (1963), Mariano Rajoy (1955)

28th March

Nicolas Hamilton (1992), Zoe Sugg (1990), Alex Wassabi (1990), Lacey Turner (1988), Jonathan Van Ness (1987), Lady Gaga (1986), Julia Stiles (1981), Nick Frost (1972), Vince Vaughn (1970)

29th March

Lucy Connell (1994), N'Golo Kanté (1991), Dimitri Payet (1987), Fabrizio Corona (1974), Elle Macpherson (1964), Amy Sedaris (1961), Jane Hawking (1944), Sam Walton (1918), John Tyler, U.S. President (1790)

30th March

David So (1987), Sergio Ramos (1986), Norah Jones (1979), Mark Consuelos (1971), Celine Dion (1968), Piers Morgan (1965), Tracy Chapman (1964), MC Hammer (1962), Robbie Coltrane (1950), Eric Clapton (1945), Vincent van Gogh (1853)

31st March

Kamilla Osman (1995), Jessica Szohr (1985), Kate Micucci (1980), Ewan McGregor (1971), Angus Young (1955), Al Gore (1948), Rhea Perlman (1948), Christopher Walken (1943), Cesar Chavez (1927), Johann Sebastian Bach (1685)

1st April

Logan Paul (1995), Ella Eyre (1994), Scotty Sire (1992), Beth Tweddle (1985), Matt Lanter (1983), Chris Evans (1966), Phillip Schofield (1962), Susan Boyle (1961), Debbie Reynolds (1932)

2nd April

Michael Fassbender (1977), Adam Rodriguez (1975), Roselyn Sanchez (1973), Linford Christie (1960), Marvin Gaye (1939), Hans Christian Anderson (1805), Giacomo Casanova (1725), King Charlemagne (742)

3rd April

Gabriel Jesus (1997), Amanda Bynes (1986), Leona Lewis (1985), Cobie Smulders (1982), Nigel Farage (1964), Eddie Murphy (1961), Alec Baldwin (1958), Jane Goodall (1934), Marlon Brando (1924), Doris Day (1922), Washington Irving (1783)

4th April

Daniel Lara (2001), Jamie Lynn Spears (1991), Todrick Hall (1985), Heath Ledger (1979), Natasha Lyonne (1979), Stephen Mulhern (1977), David Blaine (1973), Robert Downey Jr. (1965), Graham Norton (1963), Maya Angelou (1928)

5th April

Rendall Coleby (2001), Lily James (1989), Hayley Atwell (1982), Timothy Bishop (1976), Pharrell Williams (1973), Bette Davis (1908), Booker T. Washington (1856)

6th April

Peyton List (1998), Rena Lovelis (1998), Julie Ertz (1992), Myleene Klass (1978), Zach Braff (1975), Paul Rudd (1969), Louie Spence (1969), Raphael (1483)

7th April

Ellarie (1986), Ben McKee (1985), Duncan James (1978), Tiki Barber (1975), Tim Peake (1972), Russell Crowe (1964), Jackie Chan (1954), Billie Holiday (1915), William Wordsworth (1770)

8th April

Allu Arjun (1983), Gennady Golovkin (1982), Chris Kyle (1974), JR Bourne (1970), Patricia Arquette (1968), Robin Wright (1966), Vivienne Westwood (1941)

9th April

Lilia Buckingham (2003), Brooke Raboutou (2001), Elle Fanning (1998), Kristen Stewart (1990), Leighton Meester (1986), Gerard Way (1977), Marc Jacobs (1963), Dennis Quaid (1954), Hugh Hefner (1926)

10th April

Claire Wineland (1997), Daisy Ridley (1992), Alex Pettyfer (1990), Shay Mitchell (1987), Vincent Kompany (1986), Mandy Moore (1984), Sophie Ellis-Bextor (1979), Roberto Carlos (1973), Steven Seagal (1952), John Madden (1936)

11th April

Dele Alli (1996), Toddy Smith (1991), Kid Buu (1988), Michelle Phan (1987), Joss Stone (1987), Stephanie Pratt (1986), Tai Lopez (1977), Jeremy Clarkson (1960)

12th April

Katelyn Ohashi (1997), Saoirse Ronan (1994), Brendon Urie (1987), Claire Danes (1979), Christina Moore (1973), Shannen Doherty (1971), David Cassidy (1950), David Letterman (1947), Bobby Moore (1941), Jacob Zuma, South African President (1942)

13th April

Josh Gordon (1991), Allison Williams (1988), Ty Dolla $ign (1985), Claudio Bravo (1983), Carles Puyol (1978), Jonathan Brandis (1976), Ron Perlman (1950), Thomas Jefferson, U.S. President (1743)

14th April

Sarah Michelle Gellar (1977), Anderson Silva (1975), Adrien Brody (1973), Robert Carlyle (1961), Peter Capaldi (1958), Bobbi Brown (1957), Loretta Lynn (1932), Anne Sullivan (1866)

15th April

Maisie Williams (1997), Emma Watson (1990), Samira Wiley (1987), Seth Rogen (1982), Luke Evans (1979), Austin Aries (1978), Samantha Fox (1966), Emma Thompson (1959), Roy Raymond (1947), Kim Il-Sung, North Korean Premier and President (1912), Leonardo da Vinci (1452)

16th April

Sadie Sink (2002), Anya Taylor-Joy (1996), Akon (1973), Jon Cryer (1965), Martin Lawrence (1965), Kareem Abdul-Jabbar (1947), Pope Benedict XVI (1927), Charlie Chaplin (1889), Wilbur Wright (1867)

17th April

Ryland Lynch (1997), Julien Solomita (1992), Medhi Benatia (1987), Rooney Mara (1985), Victoria Beckham (1974), Jennifer Garner (1972), Sean Bean (1959), Giuseppe Zanotti (1957)

18th April

Nathan Sykes (1993), Britt Robertson (1990), Rosie Huntington-Whiteley (1987), America Ferrera (1984), Kourtney Kardashian (1979), Melissa Joan Hart (1976), David Tennant (1971), Conan O'Brien (1963), James Woods (1947), Michael D. Higgins, Irish President (1941)

19th April

Joe Hart (1987), Maria Sharapova (1987), Candace Parker (1986), Hayden Christensen (1981), Kate Hudson (1979), James Franco (1978), Ashley Judd (1968), Tim Curry (1946), Jayne Mansfield (1933)

20th April

Mirandar Kerr (1983), Joey Lawrence (1976), Carmen Electra (1972), Shemar Moore (1970), Felix Baumgartner (1969), Crispin Glover (1964), Andy Serkis (1964), Jessica Lange (1949), George Takei (1937), Joan Miró (1893), Napoleon III, French Emperor and President (1808)